# Decorative Painting Techniques
## *Whisper Painting*

# Decorative Painting Techniques
## *Whisper Painting*

### SUZY EATON

STERLING PUBLISHING CO., INC. NEW YORK

A STERLING/CHAPELLE BOOK

Chapelle, Ltd.
  P.O. Box 9252, Ogden, UT 84409
  (801) 621-2777 • (801) 621-2788 Fax
  e-mail: chapelle@chapelleltd.com
  Web site: www.chapelleltd.com

                  Library of Congress Cataloging-in-Publication Data

Eaton, Suzy.
  Decorative painting techniques : whisper painting / Suzy Eaton.
       p. cm.
  "A Sterling/Chapelle Book."
  Includes index.
  ISBN-13: 978-1-4027-2565-4
  ISBN-10: 1-4027-2565-5
  1.  House painting--Amateurs'  manuals. 2.  Furniture painting--Amateurs'
manuals.  I. Title.

TT323.E28 2006
745.7'23--dc22
                                                      2005031358

10 9 8 7 6 5 4 3 2 1
Published by Sterling Publishing Co., Inc.
387 Park Avenue South, New York, NY 10016
©2006 by Suzy Eaton
Distributed in Canada by Sterling Publishing
c/o Canadian Manda Group, 165 Dufferin Street
Toronto, Ontario, Canada M6K 3H6
Distributed in Great Britain by Chrysalis Books Group PLC,
Distributed in the United Kingdom by GMC Distribution Services,
Castle Place, 166 High Street, Lewes, East Sussex, England BN7 1XU
P.O. Box 704, Windsor, NSW 2756, Australia
Printed and Bound in China
All Rights Reserved

Sterling ISBN-13: 978-1-4027-2565-4
        ISBN-10: 1-4027-2565-5

  For information about custom editions, special sales, premium and
corporate purchases, please contact Sterling Special Sales Department at
(800) 805-5489 or specialsales@sterlingpub.

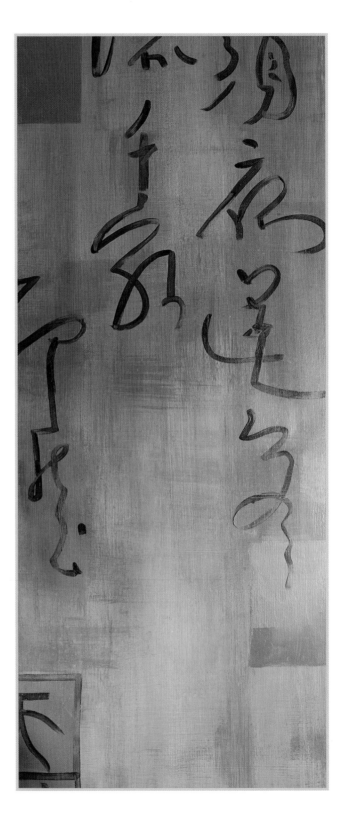

# FOREWORD
## *It's Only Paint!*

I cannot tell you how many times I have been asked by someone who so badly wants to brighten up a dull room with a painting project, "But what if I don't like it?" My response: "It's only paint!"

Paint is the cornerstone of any decorating adventure. It is the first thing that goes into a room and what sets the tone for everything else. Color can be the most powerful element in a decorating scheme if it is used well. Many people don't use color because they are afraid of making a mistake. The trick is to think about the room's function: Is it a bedroom or a bathroom? Is it dark or well lit? Is it large or small? Color has been found to be instrumental in creating certain moods, so let your emotions guide you. With the help of this book, you will have all of the necessary information to choose colors that will work for your home, reflect positive energy, and make visitors feel welcome.

Paint is inexpensive and versatile. It's easy to change wall color at will and to paint over mistakes. With the right tools, preparation, and determination, you will be able to re-create the projects throughout this book. My motto is to paint everything, as I truly believe nearly anything can be painted. Be daring and experimental. Remember, it's only paint!

# TABLE OF CONTENTS

# INTRODUCTION

Whisper painting is the art of using soft detail and faux finishing to paint your walls, furniture, or other home accessories. Subtle and oftentimes monochromatic, whisper painting does not take over the room but instead enhances it with a faint yet decorative approach to help you love the space you're in.

From the softest sponging to the trendiest applications that take on the look of fabric, suede, or leather, *Whisper Painting* offers a variety of techniques. Harlequin patterns create a lively, fashionable feel, while ragging and dragging techniques result in a time-honored style reminiscent of the past. A range of ideas for using color and pattern, combined with easy-to-follow instructions, provide a solid background for achieving the look you desire. No matter what your style, mood, or color preference, *Whisper Painting* is certain to inspire you to create your own decorative finishes, transforming your plain surface into something fabulous!

Use the paintbrush icons on each project opener page to ascertain the level of difficulty. Beginner projects have one paintbrush, intermediate projects have two paintbrushes, and advanced projects have three paintbrushes.

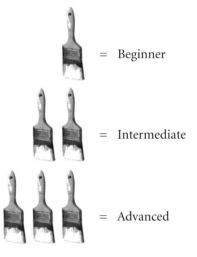

= Beginner

= Intermediate

= Advanced

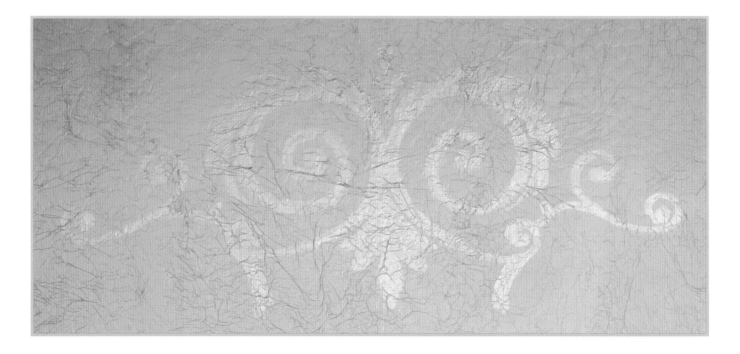

# GENERAL INFORMATION
## *Tools & Materials*

### PAINTS

There are so many types of paint available on the market that it is helpful to know a little about them. The following are paints used in some of the projects in this book. All of these paint types can easily be found at craft, home improvement, or online stores.

Acrylic latex paint, commonly known as "house paint," is a polymer-based paint that works well for walls and home interiors, but not as artist-grade paint.

Acrylic, or craft, paint is water-soluble and dries to an insoluble paint film. It is composed of pigment and an acrylic polymer emulsion, which acts as a binder.

Interference paint dries with a pearlescent finish. It is a polymer emulsion with titanium-coated mica flakes that change color when viewed at different angles. If painted over a darker color, the labeled interference color is apparent, whereas painting over a lighter color will show the complementary color.

Iridescent paint, often called "metallic paint with no metal," is a polymer emulsion with added light-absorbing colorants.

Oil paint is comprised of pigment and uses linseed oil as the binding agent. It is soluble in oil-based solvents such as turpentine or mineral spirits.

Watercolor paint is water-based and uses gum arabic as the binding agent. It becomes redissolvable once dry.

Before going to the paint store, remember to make certain to measure the room, wall, or other painting surface. This will help indicate how much paint should be purchased. Most commercially available paints cover about 400 square feet per gallon. Multiply the width of the wall by the height of the wall, then by the number of walls to be painted. Subtract any areas that will not be painted, such as windows or doors. Standard sizes are 15 square feet for windows and 21 square feet for doors.

# OTHER COMMONLY USED TOOLS & MATERIALS

The following tools and materials are used in many of the projects throughout this book.

**Artwork reproductions:** Color or black-and-white photocopies of original artwork, photographs, or other personal memorabilia are suggested to preserve the original.

**Chip brushes:** These inexpensive versatile brushes work well for a variety of techniques and with different types of paint.

**Drop cloths:** Large canvas, paper, or plastic cloths are used to protect floors and furniture while painting. Canvas drop cloths are highly absorbent, soaking up paint splatters during work time. Paper and plastic are less expensive; however, they can potentially result in paint run-offs during cleanup.

**Foam rollers:** Foam rollers work well for achieving a smooth finish on large surfaces.

**Glaze:** Glaze is used in many of these projects as it tones down the colors of the paint and allows for adequate working time.

**Level:** A level is used to ensure even surfaces and correct placement of lines.

**Masking tape:** Tape off any areas in which paint is not desired, such as electrical outlets or molding, to avoid unwanted drips or splatters.

**Paintbrushes:** A variety of paintbrushes is required, including artist's brushes as well as standard house-painting brushes.

**Paint stirrers:** Long wooden or plastic sticks are used for stirring paint. These can oftentimes be found at no cost in the paint section of the hardware store.

**Paint tray:** A slanted paint tray is helpful for holding paint when using foam rollers.

**Projector:** A projector that reflects artwork and images onto substrate is helpful for some of the projects in this book. Many art supply stores carry projectors that allow for enlarging, reducing, and color projection. An overhead projector can be substituted; however, a transparency of the artwork or pattern is required.

**Sandpaper:** 150-grit sandpaper is used for smoothing rough surfaces.

**Sea sponge:** A sea sponge is a versatile tool that can be used for paint application as well as cleanup.

**Straightedge:** A ruler or yardstick is used for drawing straight lines.

**Styrofoam applicator:** This small, hand-held tool is used for applying paint to smaller surfaces for detailed work.

# Common Painting Terminology

In addition to the materials called for throughout this book, there are some common painting terms that will be useful. They range from topics concerning color, substances added to paint for varying effects, and painting techniques to some simple general terms.

**Acetone:** Acetone is a flammable liquid used as a solvent in paints and varnishes. It can be used to clean dried acrylic paint from brushes and tools.

**Alcohol:** This solvent is used prior to acrylic paint application to decrease oily surfaces.

**Canvas:** Woven fabric is often used as a substrate for painting. It can be composed of cotton, linen, jute, and other natural or synthetic fibers. The weight refers to the thickness of the material as well as the actual weight per square yard.

**Collage:** A technique in which materials of various sizes and weights are adhered to a substrate.

**Decoupage:** A technique in which cutouts of paper, plastic, or other flat material are applied to a surface.

**Glazing:** A technique used in acrylic painting to create luminous color and depth. A glaze is created by mixing a higher ratio of gloss medium and varnish with a small amount of paint.

**Gloss:** Gloss is the shiniest, or most reflective, surface finish.

**Hue:** Synonymous with color, hue refers to the gradation of color and the properties that distinguish between colors.

**Intensity:** This refers to the brightness or strength of a color.

**Luminosity:** This term refers to the amount of light that reflects off a particular surface or color.

**Matte:** A matte surface is the dullest, or least reflective, finish.

**Medium:** A medium is an additive used to change the characteristics of paint, without affecting adhesion. For example, acrylic mediums remedy the paint useable for a variety of techniques.

**Mineral spirits:** This petroleum distillate is used to thin oil paints. Make certain to follow all package instructions, as mineral spirits can pose a toxic hazard.

**Opaque:** An opaque paint is the least transparent, and is best suited for fully covering a substrate when no transparency is desired.

**Palette:** A palette is a limited group of colors chosen for use in painting.

**Priming:** The preparation of a surface that will be painted is called priming.

**Saturation:** The degree of color intensity or vividness. A saturated color is one that is free from dilution.

**Semigloss:** Semigloss refers to the reflective properties of paint. Semigloss lies between gloss and matte finishes.

**Shade:** Shade refers to the subtle differences between gradations in color. For example, sky blue is a distinctly different shade of blue than navy.

**Shading:** Shading is used to change the value of a color, usually by adding black.

**Sheen:** This refers to the reflective quality of a dried paint surface, such as gloss, matte, or semigloss.

**Sizing:** Sizing can be used to prime the substrate so that it will be a receptive surface for paint application.

**Substrate:** A surface upon which any paint is applied, such as canvas, paper, or wood.

**Tint:** Lighter or darker shades of a color are known as tints. Generally, white can be added to create lighter tints of a particular shade.

**Tone:** This is the quality or value of a color. This term is sometimes used to describe a softening in the way the color looks.

**Translucent:** Translucent paint lies between transparent and opaque. It is suitable for both glazing and a range of other techniques.

**Transparent:** The least opaque, transparent paint is best suited for glazing techniques.

**Value:** A color value refers to luminosity and the color's relative lightness or darkness.

**Varnish:** Varnish is also known as urethane. Varnish is used on dried paint as a protective coating. It can also change the reflective nature of the color beneath the varnish, causing it to be glossy, matte, or semiglossy.

**Wash:** Composed of mostly water and a bit of paint, a wash is used in watercolor painting.

# Color Basics

Although each of the projects in this book has a color scheme listed, you might choose to use a different one, based on need or preference. Here are some thoughts on color that might be helpful to you in choosing a palette that will complement your space.

- **Red** stimulates emotions, especially those of passion and energy. It sometimes actually increases heart rate and blood pressure upon viewing.
- **Orange** evokes warmth, energy, and friendliness.
- **Yellow** is an attention-grabbing, optimistic color. It is highly visible in pure tones, so vast use of yellow as a wall color is recommended only when using softer values.
- **Green** is highly versatile. It can be experienced as both lively and relaxing, depending on the shade.
- **Blue** induces feelings of calmness and serenity.
- **Violet** is complex, arousing strong feelings of passion and creativity.

When setting out to choose which colors to use, consider these important questions. How much does a particular color appeal to your personal taste and preference? Does the color cause any feelings of unease? Do you want the room to appear larger, or perhaps more cozy?

Darker colors will cause small rooms to appear even smaller, while using a lighter color will create the illusion of more space. Cool colors will evoke calm peaceful feelings, while warm colors will intensify emotion in the room. While a particular color may appear to be exactly the right choice in the paint store, the light source in the room to be painted might cause the color to alter a bit. It is always a good idea to take paint samples home to be viewed in the desired area. Even purchasing a small amount of paint for a test patch is wise, as paint can sometimes look very different on a ceiling as opposed to a wall.

Color harmony is important for choosing paints that will look good together. Here are some common color schemes on which to base your choices.

- **Analogous** colors are those which lie next to each other on the color wheel. Blue-green, green, and yellow-green are examples of analogous colors.
- **Complementary** colors are those which lie opposite each other on the color wheel. Purple and yellow, for example, are complementary colors.
- **Monochromatic** color schemes are based on variations in lightness and saturation of a single color.

This color wheel is useful for determining what the soft and tranquil tones of whisper painting look like.

- **Bold** tones are the strongest and are highly intense.
- **Pure** tones, slightly less intense than bold, are still very vibrant.
- **Tranquil** tones begin to grow paler, but retain a bit of density.
- **Soft** tones are the palest on the wheel, and include a great deal of added white.

*Tip:*

When painting large surfaces that require more than one can of the same paint color, mix all the cans together in a larger container to ensure a consistent color.

*Cool*

*Bold*

*Pure*

*Tranquil*

*Soft*

*Soft*

*Tranquil*

*Pure*

*Bold*

*Warm*

# *Basic Techniques*

## HANDWRITING TECHNIQUE

I used to be very particular about making certain all of my artwork was completely original. I have since learned that it is not only acceptable, but sometimes necessary, to use tools and techniques to assist in making a project easier. This particular technique will save a great deal of time and frustration.

- Using any word-processing or graphics program on a computer, print the desired word or saying in the chosen font. Enlarge the saying on a photocopier, if necessary, to the desired size.

- On the back side of the paper, cover the area where the words are printed with graphite pencil, chalk, or oil pastel. A light shade of chalk is useful when transferring to a darker surface, as it will be much easier to see the image once transferred. (Fig. 1) *Note: This creates a custom carbon paper.*

- If the lettering will be painted on a straight line, use a level to pencil in a guideline to ensure even transferring. (Fig. 2) Place the paper against the wall or substrate with the graphite facing the surface. Secure the paper in place with tape. Trace around the lettering with a pen or pencil. (Fig. 3) Remove the paper from the wall. (Fig. 4)

- Thin three parts paint with one part water, as this will make the paint much easier to apply. Paint in the letters or image and allow to dry. If the words are too transparent, apply a second coat of paint. (Fig. 5)

Fig. 1

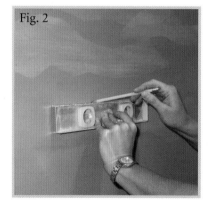

Fig. 2

Fig. 3

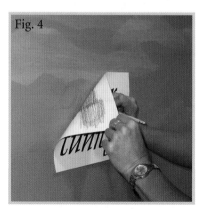

Fig. 4

Fig. 5

There is nothing better t[han]
except a good friend [...]

The Handwriting Technique on page 16 will work for any pattern
or design. Simply photocopy the wording or image
and follow the same instructions.

# DECOUPAGE TECHNIQUE

The art of decoupage is simply cutting out pictures and pasting them on furniture or home accessories to simulate painting. It is an easy craft that produces delightful results.

- Images for use in decoupage can be found just about any-where—seed catalogs, magazines, vintage books, gift wrap, wallpaper, travel brochures, greeting cards—and can be cut or torn depending on the desired effect.

- While some people prefer to use wallpaper paste for larger areas, any water-soluble paste, decoupage medium, or glue can be used. If the adhesive is very thick and could poten-tially damage delicate paper, try diluting with some water.

- Lay each image face down. Dip a brush into water, then into decoupage medium. Smoothly and evenly coat the back of the image, working from center to edges. (Fig. 1)

- Stretch the paper and press all air bubbles out when apply-ing to the surface. (Fig. 2) For large areas, a rolling pin or brayer is useful for smoothing the image out. If the edges do not stick, carefully lift and apply more decoupage medi-um with a toothpick.

- Immediately apply decoupage medium over the placed image, coating the entire surface. (Fig. 3) *Note: It is very important to cover the images with a topcoat of decoupage medium, not only to reinforce the hold but also to give the piece the desired finish.*

*Tip:*

Due to exposure to moisture, some wrinkling in the paper is inevitable; however, this will dissipate as the paper dries. A blow dryer or heat gun set on low can help eliminate wrinkling. If the decoupage project will be used outdoors or near water, seal it with varnish or similar sealant.

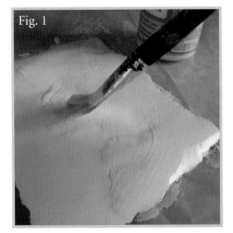

Fig. 1

Fig. 2

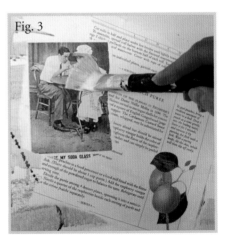

Fig. 3

The Decoupage Technique on page 18 will work for many different types of projects. This finish, for example, was created by applying pages to the wall to create book wallpaper.

# Preparation

Preparing the wall or other substrate you plan to paint is important to achieve the desired look.

Make certain to tape off any areas in which paint will not be applied. Molding and the area along floors and ceilings should be taped off to prevent drips and spills from causing permanent damage. Electrical outlets can be taped off or removed. It is also a good idea to cover furniture with tarps, or to move it away from the wall being painted.

- Cover floors with drop cloths to avoid inadvertent drips and spills.
- Wash the wall you plan to paint with a mild household cleanser.
- Rinse the wall with clean water to remove any excess cleanser.
- Sand any areas that are rough or appear to have loose paint.

- Patch any holes, dents, or cracks by pressing a small amount of spackling compound into the flawed areas and allow to dry.
- Sand spackled patches until smooth.
- Apply a base coat of primer to seal the wall and create a nonporous surface to which the paint will easily adhere.

*Tip:*

Don't worry about rinsing out each paintbrush when taking a break for an hour or two. Simply cover the bristles in plastic wrap and secure with a rubber band, or store the brush in a zip-close storage bag and place it in the freezer.

# Cleanup

- Latex paint can be cleaned off brushes and tools, using soap and water. Oil-based paints should be removed using paint thinner, making certain to follow the package directions.

- Petroleum jelly can be used instead of masking tape to protect doorknobs and windows from paint drips.

- Accidental latex paint drips can be removed by dabbing them with vinegar. If the paint drip is on the carpet, don't wipe it up or it may smear. Allow the paint to dry, then cut the paint drips out with scissors.

- Always store brushes laying down flat or hanging up. Avoid storing the brush standing on its bristles, as this will shorten the life of the brush.

*Tip:*

Instead of throwing away leftover paint or other materials, donate them to a community arts center, playhouse, or high school drama department. Many groups could use the paint for public murals or for painting sets for local productions.

# SECTION 1
## *The Projects*
## *Metallic Tissue Paper Wall*

This is a great way to add texture and color to a wall without overwhelming the room. Flaws or irregularities can be easily covered using the inexpensive everyday items. This elegant wall treatment will enrich any space with depth and sheen.

## MATERIALS LIST:

- Latex paint, color of choice
- Masking tape
- Metallic paint, color of choice
- Paint roller
- Paint stirrers
- Paint tray
- Roller covers
- Styrofoam applicator
- Tissue paper, white
- Translucent glaze

*Continued on page 24*

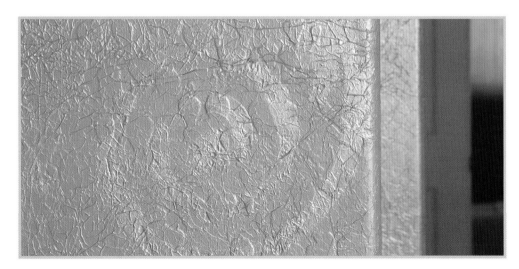

*Continued from page 22*

*Note: It is not necessary to paint the wall the desired color before beginning the project, as the combination of paint and tissue will be adequate.*

Step 1.  Separate tissue sheets and crumple each individually.

Step 2.  Mix one part latex paint to one part glaze. *Note: Mixing the glaze in with the paint will allow more time to work before the paint dries.*

Step 3.  Working in 3'-square sections, roll the paint/glaze mixture onto the wall.

Step 4.  Flatten out the crumpled tissue and press into the wet paint, making certain it is completely adhered. *Note: It is critical that the paint not dry before the tissue paper is applied.* Roll over the tissue paper with a second coat of the paint/glaze mixture, allowing crinkles and folds to form.

Step 5.  Continue applying tissue randomly, overlapping each piece so the entire wall is covered. Roll more paint/glaze mixture over the applied tissue paper. Allow to dry completely, for at least eight hours.

Step 6.  Mix one part metallic paint to two parts glaze.

Step 7.  Using the Styrofoam applicator, wipe the metallic paint/glaze mixture over the entire tissue-covered wall. Allow the metallic glaze to fill in the folds and cracks.

*Tip:*

I added a few decorative scroll patterns to complete the look I wanted for this room; however, your wall will look great with or without the extra detail. See photograph on page 23.

Step 2

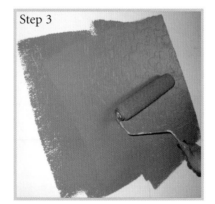

Step 3

Step 4a

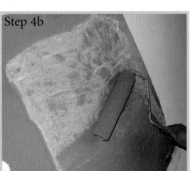

Step 4b

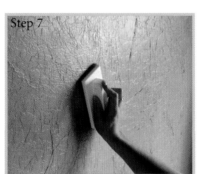

Step 7

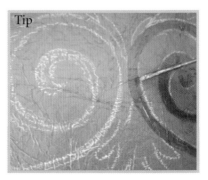

Tip

# Artist's Textured Wall

This is a wild, free-form wall that just seemed to fit into my art studio. There is really no right or wrong way to do it, just be creative and have fun.

## MATERIALS LIST:

- Assorted wood pieces
- Flat trowel
- Glass shards
- Hammer (optional)
- Industrial-strength adhesive
- Latex paint
- Marbles
- Nail (optional)
- Notched trowel
- Paint rags
- Paint tray
- Paintbrush, 3"
- Patching plaster
- Soldering wire, .125 gauge
- Wire cutters

*Continued on page 28*

*Continued from page 26*

**Step 1.** Using the flat trowel, apply ⅛"–¼"-thick patching plaster in 4'-square sections to the wall. *Note: Although most of the wall should be covered with patching plaster, some areas can be left bare in order to let the original wall color show through.*

**Step 2.** Pull the notched trowel through a few of the wet areas to create a design of textured lines. Use finger to draw designs and words.

**Step 3.** Press glass shards, marbles, and wood pieces into the remaining wet areas of patching plaster. *Note: If some of the accent pieces are too large to attach at this point, wait until after the wall is painted. I did not want to make my wall too busy, but wanted to add in a few colors here and there.* Allow to dry for 24 hours.

**Step 4.** Thin two parts latex paint with one part water. Use the paintbrush to fill in all bumps and cracks, working in sections.

**Step 5.** Using a wet paint rag, begin to wipe off small amounts of paint in some areas and more in other areas, creating a varied look. Rinse out the rag occasionally, and continue until the entire wall has been painted and wiped to the desired effect. Allow to dry.

**Step 6.** Glue remaining large pieces to wall.

**Step 7.** Bend soldering wire into an inspirational word. Adhere it to the wall, or nail it in place.

*Tip:*
Scour flea markets and dollar stores for colored drinking glasses or flower vases. It can be great fun to smash them up at home, just remember to wear appropriate safety gear such as gloves and eyewear.

Step 1

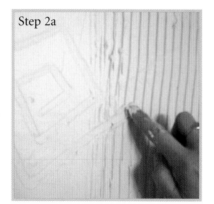
Step 2a

Step 2b

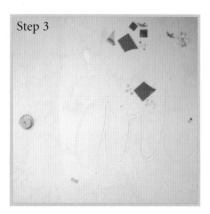
Step 3

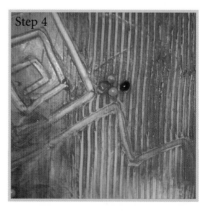
Step 4

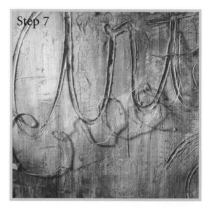
Step 7

# Texture Magic Mantel

Texture can be a great way to add detail to a plain surface. This project is so easy and fun and will transform something very dull and flat into an inexpensive elegant showpiece. This technique can be used in a small area such as this, or over an entire wall.

## MATERIALS LIST:

- Dimensional paint, color of choice
- Masking tape
- Metallic glaze, gold
- Paper plate
- Pencil
- Sea sponge
- Spackle knife, 6"
- Stencil

*Continued on page 32*

This elegant piece incorporates both the subtle detail of the Texture Magic Mantel on page 30 and the cozy fire of the Canvas Mural on page 34.

*Continued from page 30*

Step 1.  Tape the stencil in desired portion of mantel.

Step 2.  Squeeze dimensional paint onto a paper plate.

Step 3.  Using the spackle knife, evenly spread dimensional paint over the stencil.

Step 4.  Carefully remove the stencil and tape in the next spot on the mantel. Continue this process until your design is finished.

Step 5.  Allow to dry for approximately four hours.

Step 6.  Wet the sea sponge and wring until damp. Dip into the gold metallic glaze and cover the stenciled design, allowing the glaze to catch the edges of the design. *Note: If you feel the color is too dark, use the opposite side of the sponge to wipe off glaze to desired effect.*

Step 7.  Subtly glaze the rest of mantel with metallic gold to blend in with the stenciled design. *Note: For this project, I used a darker color of dimensional paint for demonstration purposes, then painted it off-white.*

*Tip:*

**A plethora of fun combinations can result with various dimensional paint, latex, and acrylic paint colors**

Step 1

Step 2

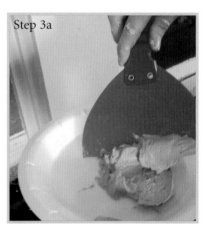

Step 3a

Step 3b

Step 4

Step 6

# Canvas Mural

This plain wall was transformed by building a charming mantel, then adding a faux fire to give it a realistic feel. This technique creates a nice hand-painted piece.

## MATERIALS LIST:

- Acrylic paints, assorted colors to match chosen photograph or picture
- Artist's paintbrushes, assorted sizes
- Canvas, sized to fit project area
- Construction glue
- Joint compound
- Photograph
- Sandpaper
- Spackle knife, 6"
- Tack cloth

Step 1. Choose a photograph or picture to be used as a mural. Have the image enlarged to fit your project and reproduced onto canvas.

Step 2. Apply construction glue to the back of the canvas, spreading thoroughly to cover entire surface. Make certain to adequately apply adhesive to the edges and corners, so that they do not droop once the canvas is hung. Adhere canvas to the wall.

Step 3. Immediately following placement of the canvas, use the spackle knife to apply a thin coat of joint compound around the edges of the canvas. Allow to dry for three to four hours.

Step 4. Apply a second coat, feathering out the joint compound a bit farther. Allow to dry. *Note: The goal is to blend the canvas into the wall, so there are no hard lines visible.* Sand until the joint compound creates a smooth transition.

Step 5. Apply a third coat, if necessary. Allow to dry and sand smooth.

Step 6. Using tack cloth, wipe off any drywall dust from artwork and surrounding area, as it will interfere with your painting.

Step 7. Paint over the printed canvas piece, following the photograph or picture.

*Tip:*

As the chosen photograph is simply a guide for painting the mural, try toning down or changing colors that don't work for your individual project.

Step 1

Step 2a

Step 2b

Step 2c

Step 3

Step 7

# Renaissance Antiqued Mirror

This technique turns a brand-new mirror into something that looks like it has been around for centuries. It can be hung as more than just a mirror, but as a work of art as well.

## MATERIALS LIST:

- Artwork reproduction
- Bronzing powders: aluminum, brass, pale gold
- Chip paintbrushes
- Craft paper
- Decoupage medium
- Glass bowl
- Latex gloves
- Mirror
- Muratic acid
- Paint stripper
- Paintbrushes
- Painter's mask
- Paper towels
- Plastic scraper
- Sizing
- Spray paint, black

*Continued on page 38*

*Continued from page 36*

Step 1.  Turn mirror face down on craft paper and, following manufacturer's instructions, apply paint stripper to mirror back to remove protective coating. Rinse with clean water and allow to dry.

Step 2.  Wearing a mask and latex gloves, pour muratic acid into a glass bowl. Crumple up a paper towel, dip into acid, and rub over the entire mirror back. *Note: This will cause the acid to streak and bead up in areas.* Wait five minutes.

Step 3.  Repeat Step 2, until the silvering begins to rub off. The silvering will not begin to disappear until the acid is rubbed against it. Once this happens, rub off small amounts all over the mirror, then immediately wash off the mirror with water. Dry with a paper towel to prevent further deterioration. *Note: Do not remove all of the silvering.*

Step 4.  Tear the edges of the artwork reproduction. Tear into a few smaller pieces.

Step 5.  Select a spot on the mirror that has more of the silvering removed, and determine if this is a good area to permanently position the artwork.

Step 6.  Paint a coat of decoupage medium onto the front of the artwork reproduction and apply to mirror back. Paint a coat of decoupage medium onto the back of the artwork, as well, repeating this process until the desired composition is achieved. Allow to dry.

Step 7.  Paint a coat of sizing over the entire mirror back. Allow to dry until tacky, for approximately one-half hour.

Step 8.  Wearing the mask, sprinkle bronzing powder over sizing. Then sprinkle some aluminum and finish up with the gold. Using a clean dry paintbrush, spread over the back of the entire mirror. Brush off any excess powder.

Step 9.  Spray the back of the mirror with black paint.

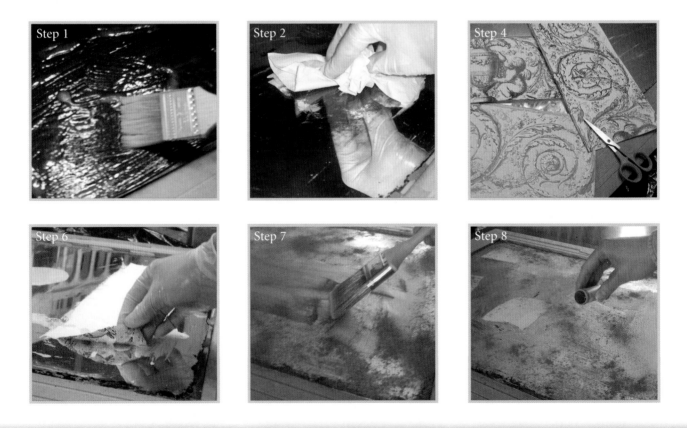

This mirror was antiqued using the same process described for Renaissance Antiqued Mirror on page 36. However, this version does not have decoupage across the back. The front functions as a bulletin board, displaying personal family photos of special memories.

# *Oriental Sheer*

This project exemplifies the idea that paint need not be applied strictly to walls and furniture. When the paint is thinned with water, it can be applied to fabric without drying stiff, yet still be washable and durable. The paint also becomes translucent, which is perfect for this project.

## MATERIALS LIST:

- Acrylic paint, color of choice
- Artist's paintbrush, #3
- Artwork reproduction
- Masking tape
- Paint tray
- Sheer curtain panel(s)
- Straight pins

*Continued on page 42*

*Continued from page 40*

Step 1.   Enlarge artwork to desired size on a photocopier. *Note: There is no need to reproduce it in color, as it will be used only as a pattern.*

Step 2.   Beginning in a corner, place the sheer over the pattern and pin it down.

Step 3.   Mix two parts paint to one part water.

Step 4.   Dip the brush into the paint, wiping off any excess. Paint over the pattern lines. Allow to dry. *Note: It is imperative that the paint dry before separating the sheer from the pattern, as the paint will run if removed too soon.*

Step 5.   Move pattern to a new area and continue painting.

*Note: Designs that work well for this project are patterns that repeat themselves, as they are more easily matched up when moved around.*

*Tip:*

A design with a repeating pattern can be photocopied several times and enlarged or reduced as desired. Taped together, the photocopies make one large pattern that does not have to be unpinned and moved around.

Step 1a

Step 1b

Step 2

Step 4

# Artichoke Headboard

One thing I often try when beginning a new project is to do the unexpected, whether I am painting or decorating. In this case, the attic bedroom with dormer windows and side rooms demands to be different. The bed is right at home in the middle of the room, and because of this, exposes the back side of the headboard, which just begs to be painted.

## MATERIALS LIST:

- Acrylic paints, colors of choice
- Artist's paintbrushes, assorted sizes
- Latex paint, color of choice
- Paper plates
- Satin water-based polyurethane
- Styrofoam applicator
- Translucent glaze
- Water-based wood stains, colors to match chosen headboard
- Wooden headboard

Although this headboard is a sturdy, high-quality piece of furniture, the back was simply plywood stained the same color as the front. As it was never meant to be exposed, it just did not look finished. For this reason, I decided to faux finish the plywood to look a bit more like the rich stained wood on the front of the headboard. I have included the Artichoke Template on page 46 so you can photocopy and trace it onto your own project if you so choose.

Step 1. Apply latex paint as the base coat, in order to create deep golden undertones. Allow to dry for approximately one hour.

Step 2. Using the Styrofoam applicator, apply a layer of wood stain. *Note: Using the Styrofoam applicator will allow for more control over how much stain is applied.*

*It will also begin to give the look of wood grain lines, which will be necessary in the layering process.*

Step 3. Layers need not be too precise, as some areas should be slightly more covered than others. Allow to dry.

Step 4. Apply second color of wood stain, using the same technique described in Step 2. Allow to dry.

Step 5. Repeat with third color of wood stain.

Step 6. Trace or draw artichoke pattern onto headboard.

Step 7. Pour translucent glaze into the center of a paper plate. Pour small amounts of each paint color around the glaze. Drag glaze into each color as the paint is applied. *Note: The more glaze used, the more transparent the artwork will appear.*

*Continued on page 46*

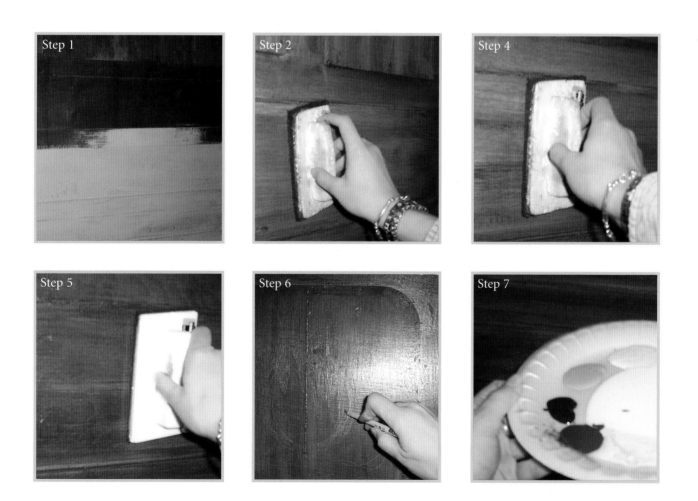

*Continued from page 44*

Step 8.   Begin with the background and build up. Apply the darkest colors, then highlight with lighter colors, remembering to mix each color with glaze.

Step 9.   Paint the remaining artichokes, using the same technique described in Step 8. Allow to dry.

Step 10.  Apply another coat of the second stain, using the Styrofoam applicator. Cover everything except the artwork; however, a minor amount of overlapping can occur near the edges, so that the artwork blends more easily onto the wood. Allow to dry.

Step 11.  Mix equal parts of the third wood stain with satin polyurethane.

Step 12.  Apply stain/polyurethane mixture to entire back of headboard, using the Styrofoam applicator. *Note: This will tone down the colors, making the artichoke subtler, while protecting the entire piece.*

Step 8

Step 9

Step 9

**Artichoke Template**

Enlarge or reduce as desired.

# Ancestral Armoire

 Unlike other furniture refinishing projects, there is no need to sand down or strip off the varnish or stain from the armoire before painting. Simply clean or dust it first, and you're ready to begin.

## MATERIALS LIST:

- Armoire
- Correspondence letters printed on transfer paper
- Crackle medium
- Iron, heated to medium setting
- Latex paint, off-white
- Metallic glaze, gold

- Paint roller
- Paintbrushes, 3"
- Papers: handmade, watercolor, or other fibrous texture
- Photographs printed on transfer paper
- Satin water-based varnish (optional)
- Sea sponge

Step 1. Paint crackle medium over entire armoire. Allow to dry until just tacky.

Step 2. Carefully paint entire armoire off-white. *Note: Take care not to overbrush, as the painted areas will immediately begin to crackle. Painting over these areas again will disturb the crackling process.* Allow to dry for three to four hours.

Step 3. Tear edges of fibrous paper to the size that will work best for chosen photos and letters.

Step 4. Roll satin varnish over a small section of the armoire.

Step 5. Randomly apply fibrous paper pieces to the wet surface of the armoire, 8"–12" apart. Seal the paper with one more coat of varnish. Allow to dry.

Step 6. Iron-transfer the images directly onto the paper that has been sealed to the armoire. *Note: If the iron is too hot, it will cause the paint to peel.* Allow to dry.

Step 7. Wet the sea sponge and dip into the off-white paint. Coat the images with a "white wash," to tone them down a bit. Allow to dry.

Step 8. Repeat Step 7 with gold metallic glaze, covering entire armoire, including images. *Note: This will give the armoire and your images an antiqued finish.*

Step 9. Seal armoire with satin varnish, if desired.

*Tips:*

I prefer to take all the hinges and hardware off before I begin, as it's easier than trying to tape them all off. Remember, the direction in which you apply the crackle medium is the direction in which it will crack. I painted my armoire with up and down strokes, in order to achieve vertical cracks.

Step 1

Step 2

Step 6a

Step 6b

Step 7

# Music Room

This wall finish is meant to look like an old piece of sheet music. A fairly simple technique to master, this wall will create an elegant feel for any room in your home.

## MATERIALS LIST:

- Image projector
- Latex paints: brown, cream
- Paint roller
- Paint tray
- Round paintbrush, #3
- Sheet music
- Translucent glaze

Step 1. Pour two parts cream paint into the paint tray and pour one part brown directly into the middle of the cream.

Step 2. Roll paint roller across tray, picking up both colors. Roll onto wall until just covered. Be certain not to overwork the paint, as the goal is to see both of the colors. Too much rolling will blend the colors together. Allow to dry completely.

Step 3. Project sheet music onto the wall. *Note: The darker the room, the easier it will be to see the projection.*

Step 4. Mix one part brown with one part glaze. Using the paintbrush, paint the sheet music onto the wall.

*Tip:*

To help make cleanup a bit easier, try lining the paint tray with a plastic garbage sack before pouring the paint. Once the wall is finished, simply throw out the garbage liner.

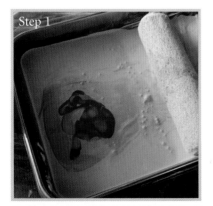

Step 1

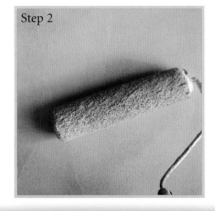

Step 2

Step 4

# Asian Linen

Asian interiors generally use neutral, natural colors to provide a simple background, which creates a relaxing monochromatic feel. Eastern art colors are pure and original. This means the initial color and/or brush stroke is the final result. It is simple, strong, and graphic. Using these philosophies will create a truly Eastern ambience in your home.

## MATERIALS LIST:

- Acrylic paints: black, burnt umber
- Artist's paintbrushes: #2, #11
- Chip paintbrush, large
- Image projector
- Latex paints, three colors of choice
- Level
- Metallic glaze, gold
- Paintbrush, 3"
- Paper plates
- Pencil
- Photocopy of Asian characters
- Styrofoam applicator
- Translucent glaze

*Continued on page 54*

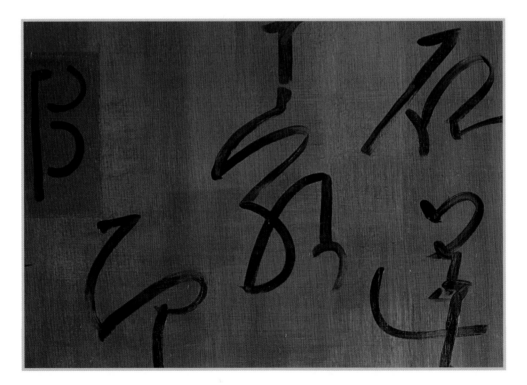

*Continued from page 52*

Step 1. Pour a bit of each latex paint color onto separate paper plates.

Step 2. Using the Styrofoam applicator, pick up a bit of one paint color. Pressing in a downward motion, apply paint to the majority of the wall, leaving a few random spots uncovered.

Step 3. Pick up a small amount of the second paint color. Randomly apply in some of both the painted and unpainted sections.

Step 4. Repeat this process with the third color, then the translucent glaze.

Step 5. Work all colors until a horizontal, streaked look is achieved. Allow to dry.

Step 6. Mix one part burnt umber acrylic paint with six parts translucent glaze. Working in sections from top to bottom, use the 3" paintbrush to apply glaze to the wall.

Step 7. Drag the chip brush through the glaze in a vertical motion from ceiling to floor at random intervals along the entire wall. Repeat this process, making horizontal lines, so that the crisscross pattern resembles that of linen. Allow to dry.

Step 8. Using a level, draw a few randomly placed squares on the wall. Using the #11 paintbrush, paint the squares with metallic glaze. Allow to dry.

Step 9. Project Asian characters onto the wall. *Note: The darker the room, the easier it will be to see the artwork.*

Step 10. Mix one part black paint with one part glaze. Using the #2 paintbrush, paint the lettering onto the wall. Paint characters in a few of the gold boxes. Allow to dry completely.

Step 11. Dip the chip brush into the gold metallic glaze, brushing over the lettering in both vertical and horizontal strokes, just until the painting becomes a bit subtler. *Note: In order to keep in line with the "whisper painting" theme, you will want to tone down the lettering somewhat.*

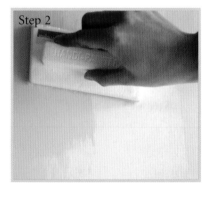

Step 2

Step 3

Step 6

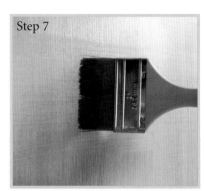

Step 7

Step 8

Step 10

# Unfinished Mural

This mural is meant to look like a work in progress. The measuring lines and smudges are left as part of the drawing, while the paint purposely moves outside the lines.

## MATERIALS LIST:

- Acrylic paints, assorted colors to match chosen artwork
- Adhesive thinner
- Artwork
- Artist's paintbrushes, assorted sizes
- Chalk, raw sienna
- Cloth
- Colored pencil, raw sienna
- Cotton balls
- Latex paints, two colors of choice
- Masking tape
- Paper plates
- Plastic container
- Satin water-based polyurethane (optional)
- Styrofoam applicator
- Tape measure
- Translucent glaze

**Chalked Artwork Instructions**

Step 1. Find or draw the artwork desired for mural.

Step 2. Measure the wall onto which the mural will be painted.

Step 3. Have artwork enlarged to the size of the wall. *Note: I used a pattern that repeats itself, and divided the 6' x 9' wall by four. The pattern was then printed on four 3' x 4½' sheets, which I then pieced together.*

Step 4. Cover the entire back of the artwork with chalk.

Step 5. Pour some adhesive thinner into a container. Saturate a cotton ball and wipe all over the chalk, turning it from a powder into a liquid. *Note: The adhesive thinner will dry very quickly, rendering it less complicated to work with; however, it will still function as a transfer material.*

Step 6. Roll up the artwork, chalk side in, and set aside for future use.

**Mural Instructions**

Step 7. Paint the wall the desired background color. Allow to dry.

Step 8. Mix one part accent color with one part translucent glaze. *Note: This is the paint color you will use to attain the cloudy effect around the border of the mural.*

Step 9. Beginning at the top and working in 4'-square sections, dab paint/glaze mixture around the outside edges of the wall with a paintbrush.

*Continued on page 58*

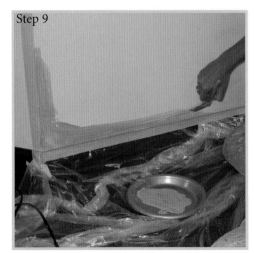

*Continued from page 56*

**Step 10.** Using a Styrofoam applicator, spread the accent paint in a circular motion, blending toward the center of the wall. *Note: This will create an effect of the accent color fading into the background wall color.*

**Step 11.** Dampen the Styrofoam applicator tip with water, squeezing out as much excess water as possible. Using the same circular motion, blend the edges of the accent color toward the main color again. *Note: This will create finer lines and a smoother transition.* Allow to dry.

**Step 12.** Beginning at the top of the wall, tape up the prepared design. Using a pen or pencil, trace over the artwork, transferring it to the wall.

**Step 13.** Remove taped artwork from the wall.

**Step 14.** Decide which areas of the mural will be painted. Begin painting, starting with the simplest parts and ending with the finest details. Leave the outside edges of the mural unpainted, as it will add to the "unfinished" look of the mural. Allow to dry.

**Step 15.** Use the colored pencil to draw over the lines on the unpainted parts of the mural.

**Step 16.** Using a wet cloth, gently wipe away the chalk lines, being careful not to wipe away the colored pencil. *Note: The colored pencil will create a sketched look for the mural. To acquire a slightly more "finished" look, use paint pens instead of pencil.*

Optional: Seal the wall with water-based polyurethane to avoid smudging when the wall is touched or cleaned.

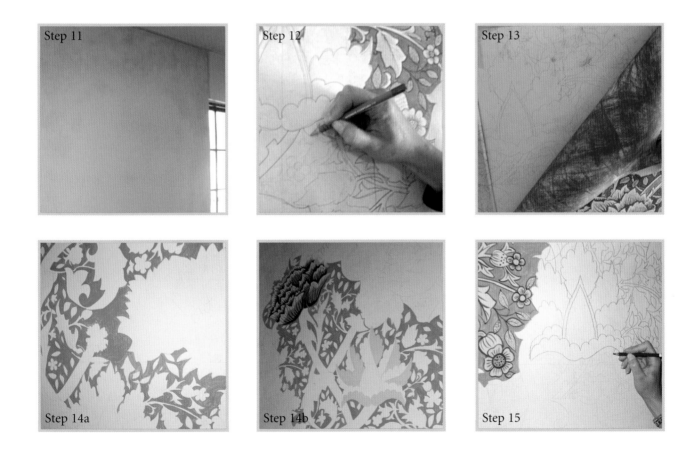

Step 11

Step 12

Step 13

Step 14a

Step 14b

Step 15

# Greek Architecture

Think of this project as a giant canvas, as it will essentially be a large painting. Cloudy, blended brushstrokes create a feeling of museum-quality impressionistic painting.

## MATERIALS LIST:

- Artist's paintbrushes, assorted sizes
- Artwork
- Image projector
- Latex paints, three colors of choice
- Oil pastel, burnt umber
- Paint roller
- Paint tray
- Paintbrush, 3"
- Satin water-based varnish

*Continued on page 62*

650        c. 575  c. 550  c. 530      490 480                    to 323 B.C. →

s |                 Francois  EXEKIAS  Peplos      Battle | Kritios
rod →    |           Vase     Dionysos  Kore        of   | Boy
         |                    In a Sailboat       Marathon

RCHA    C      P  E  R  I  O  D                      CLASSICAL
                                                     PERIOD

                        IONIC ORDER

KINGCORNICE

CORNICE

                        ⎫
                   FRIEZE ⎬          ⎫
                        ⎭           ⎪
           ⎫ ARCHITRAVE            ⎬ ENTABLATURE
    FACIAE ⎬ OR EPISTYLE           ⎪
    ABACUS ⎭                        ⎭
VOLUTE  ⎫ CAPITAL
        ⎬                           ⎫
        ⎭                           ⎪
         SHAFT                      ⎬ COLUMN
                                    ⎪
         BASE                       ⎭

         STYLOBATE

*Continued from page 60*

**Step 1.** Begin by brushing the three paint colors onto the wall, feathering them in together. *Note: I painted the first color in the upper-right corner, allowing it to cover about one-third of the wall. I then blended in the second color, covering about one-quarter of the wall. Last, I painted on the final color, which was used just as an accent.* Moving toward the bottom of the wall, repeat this step until the entire wall is covered and has a cloudy look. Allow to dry completely.

**Step 2.** Project chosen artwork onto the wall. *Note: The darker the room, the easier it will be to see your artwork.*

**Step 3.** Using the oil pastel, trace the image onto the wall.

**Step 4.** *Note: Because the images are a bit dark for the wall, it is necessary to place a light wash over the artwork.* Mix one part of the first latex paint color to two parts water. Using the 3" paintbrush, lightly paint over all of the drawn images. *Note: As oil pastels are very soft, take care* not to apply too much pressure or they may smear. Allow to dry.

**Step 5.** Using the paint roller, seal the wall with a gently applied coat of water-based varnish. *Note: If the wall is not sealed, the oil pastels will rub off when touched.* Allow to dry.

*Tip:*

Keep a bucket of water on hand. Dip your brush and wipe away any excess water before moving to the paint. This will thin out the color, making it easier to feather the paint together.

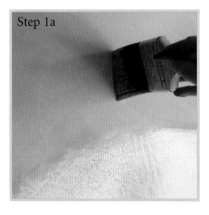
Step 1a

Step 1b

Step 1c

Step 3a

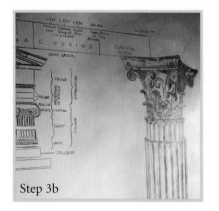
Step 3b

Step 4

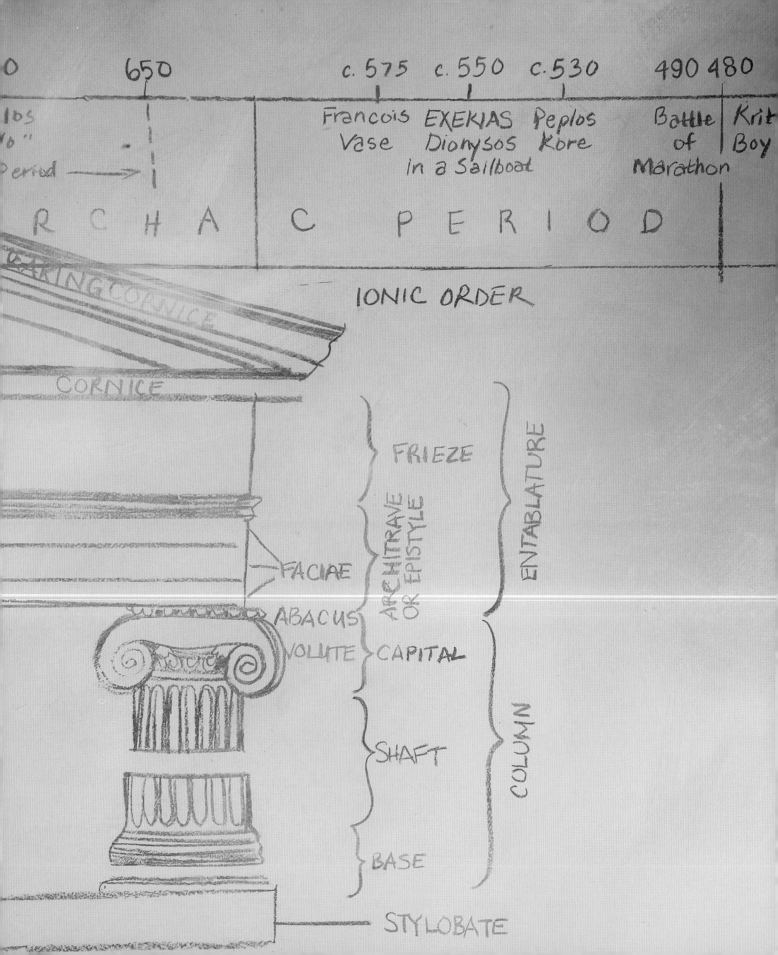

| O | 650 | | c. 575 | c. 550 | c. 530 | 490 480 |
|---|---|---|---|---|---|---|
| los | | | Francois EXEKIAS Peplos | | | Battle Krit |
| "o " | | | Vase Dionysos Kore | | | of Boy |
| Period ⟶ | | | in a Sailboat | | | Marathon |

A R C H A I C   P E R I O D

IONIC ORDER

- RAKING CORNICE
- CORNICE
- FASCIAE
- ABACUS
- VOLUTE
- FRIEZE
- ARCHITRAVE OR EPISTYLE
- ENTABLATURE
- CAPITAL
- SHAFT
- COLUMN
- BASE
- STYLOBATE

# Metallic Harlequin Wall

This wall has turned out to be one of my all-time favorites. I created it for a teenage girl who wanted a fun, unique room to bring her friends to.

## MATERIALS LIST:

- Chalk line
- Cloth
- Foam roller, 4"
- Industrial-strength adhesive
- Interference paint, violet
- Jewels
- Latex paints: dark purple, light purple, silver, violet

- Level
- Masking tape, 2"-wide
- Metallic glaze, silver
- Paintbrushes, assorted sizes
- Pencil
- Razor blade
- Ruler or yardstick
- Tape measure

*Continued on page 66*

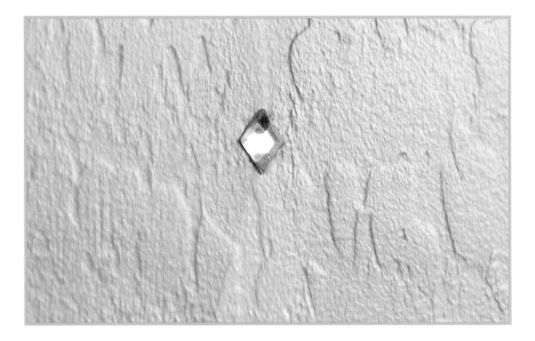

*Continued from page 64*

Step 1. Paint the entire wall violet. Allow to dry.

Step 2. Measure the width of the wall, dividing into as many equal parts as desired. *Note: I suggest making each portion no less than 16" wide. The wall I used measured 145½", which I divided by nine to make my dividers 16⅟₁₆" apart.*

Step 3. Begin on one side of the wall and mark each measurement along the ceiling. Repeat this step along the floor, making certain to begin on the same side of the wall as the ceiling was marked to ensure the marks line up.

Step 4. Using the chalk line, begin in the upper-left corner. Have an assistant count over three lines to the right and snap a diagonal line. You and your helper move one mark to the right, snapping diagonal lines until the end of the wall is reached.

Step 5. Switch to the upper-right corner, and repeat Step 4, moving toward the left. (Fig. 1) *Note: There is now an area along both the right and left side of the wall where there are no markers to indicate where the chalk needs to be snapped.*

Step 6. Place the level horizontally through the cross section of the diamonds nearest the floor, and lightly mark the spot where the level meets the wall. Move upward until the ceiling is reached and repeat on the opposite side of the wall. Using these marks as indicators, snap the remaining chalk lines. (Fig. 2)

Step 7. Tape off the inside of every other diamond. Use the razor blade to remove any overlapping tape.

*Continued on page 68*

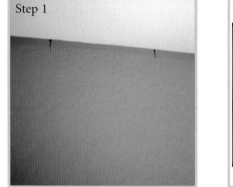
Step 1

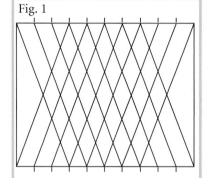
Fig. 1

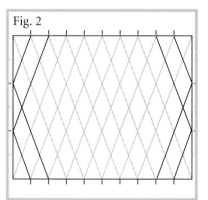
Fig. 2

Step 7a

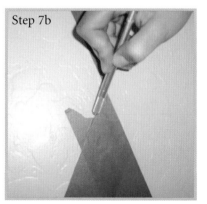
Step 7b

*Continued from page 66*

**Step 8.** Alternating between light purple, dark purple, and silver, randomly paint in the diamonds that are not taped. Allow to dry.

**Step 9.** Remove all tape from the wall. Randomly choose a few light purple, dark purple, and violet diamonds to accentuate by painting over these colors with interference violet. *Note: The interference violet will slightly alter the color underneath, while adding sparkle to the wall.* Allow to dry.

**Step 10.** Using wet cloth, clean up any remaining chalk lines.

**Step 11.** Tape off the outside edge of three or four large diamonds consisting of four small diamonds. (Fig. 3)

**Step 12.** Using silver metallic glaze, paint over the four diamonds to form one large diamond. Allow to dry.

**Step 13.** Enlarge or reduce the Diamond Template on a photocopier as desired. *Note: My larger diamonds measured 15" x 38", so I made my diamond template 7½" x 19".* Place this template in random areas on the wall, and lightly trace around using a pencil. Paint in the template-sized diamonds with silver paint. Allow to dry.

**Step 14.** Using industrial-strength adhesive, randomly secure jewels to wall where diamond points meet.

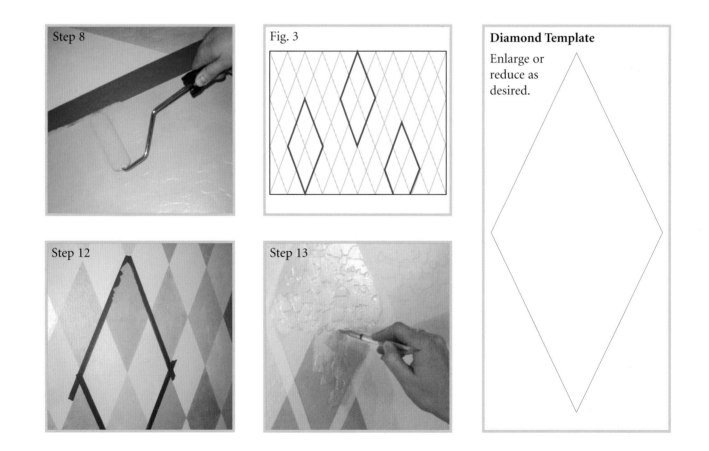

Step 8

Fig. 3

**Diamond Template**
Enlarge or reduce as desired.

Step 12

Step 13

Art Supplies

# Aged Stone Wall

One of the most requested wall finishes I am asked to create is aged stone, block, or brick. It is relatively easy and very forgiving for painting errors. They are really just sponged framework with simple shading. The tedious aspect of this wall is laying out your pattern, figuring out the size of the bricks, and marking them. However, with the right tools, this project will prove to be painless.

## MATERIALS LIST:

- Cloth
- Foam roller, small
- Household cleaner
- Latex paints, five lighter colors and two darker colors of choice
- Level
- Masking tape
- Paint trays

- Paintbrushes, assorted sizes
- Paper plates
- Pencil
- Sea sponges
- Spackle knife, 6"
- Tape measure or ruler
- Translucent glaze

*Continued on page 72*

Continued from page 70

Step 1.  Measure the wall from floor to ceiling to determine what size the bricks will be. *Note: My wall is 96", or 8', tall, so I want to make my bricks 12" tall. I will leave ½" for the mortar, so each brick will be 11½" tall. Begin with a wall that is a neutral gray, off-white, or light beige, as this will act as the mortar color between the bricks.*

Step 2.  Measure the width of the wall to determine the width of each brick. *Note: I want my bricks to be quite wide, so they will be 23½" with a ½" mortar line.*

Step 3.  To make the brick pattern even on both sides, begin in the middle of the wall and work out to either side. As blocks, bricks, and stones are always stacked so that the mortar lines up on every other row, be certain to draw them in that pattern. In other words, line up rows 1, 3, 5, etc., and 2, 4, 6, etc. (Fig. 1) Measure carefully and use the level to ensure you are penciling in straight lines.

Step 4.  Draw the ½" mortar lines on the bottom and left side of each brick. (Fig. 2) *Note: If you draw mortar lines on all four sides of your bricks, you will end up with 1" lines.*

Step 5.  Tape off wall edges, floor, and ceiling. *Note: Mortar lines can also be taped off to prevent drips; however, not using tape will allow the bricks to have a more jagged, realistic edge.*

Step 6.  Pour the lighter paint colors all into the same tray, allowing the colors to run together only a bit.

Step 7.  Use the foam roller and randomly pick up two or three colors at a time, alternating colors with each brick. Roll inside of the drawn brick, defining the edges. Roll just enough to color in the bricks, other-wise the paint colors will run together. *Note: The variation in colors will help it to look like real stone.* Continue this process until all of the bricks are filled in. Allow to dry.

Step 8.  In two separate paint trays, mix equal parts translucent glaze with each of the darker paint colors. Pour a small amount of each paint/glaze mixture onto one paper plate.

Continued on page 74

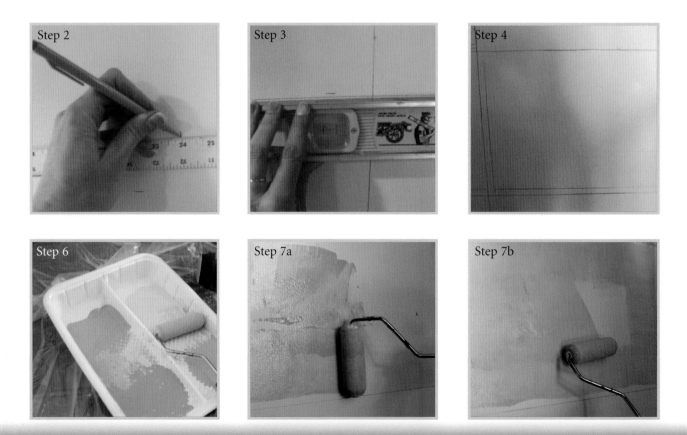

72

Fig. 1

Fig. 2

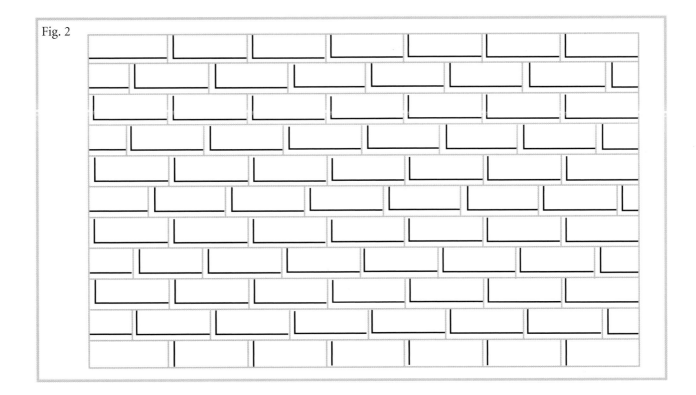

*Continued from page 72*

**Step 9.** Dampen the sea sponge and use it to pick up a dab of each color, again alternating the amount and color combination. Dab paint all over the bricks. If too much paint is applied, turn the sponge over and lightly dab excess away. As these are just accent colors, it is not necessary to cover the entire brick. Randomly apply all over each brick, lighter in some areas and darker in others. Allow to dry thoroughly, for approximately one hour.

**Step 10.** Using a household cleaner, clean all pencil lines from the wall.

**Step 11.** Mix one part of the lightest paint color, preferably an off-white shade, with one part translucent glaze. Using a clean damp sponge, spread over the entire wall, leaving a light wash. *Note: This will help tone down the harshness of some of the paint used, giving the stones an aged look.* Make certain to not press too hard, as this could potentially remove some of the accents or shadow lines.

**Step 12.** Shading is necessary to give the bricks some dimension. Choose a direction from which a natural light source might hit the wall. *Note: If the light source comes from the left, the shadow line should be painted along the right side and base of each brick.* Mix a small amount of the darkest accent color with water at a one to two ratio. Hand-paint the shadows in. *Note: Don't worry if the lines are a bit jagged. This will make the shadows more natural looking.*

**Step 13.** Mix one part of the lightest paint color with one part glaze and pour onto a paper plate. Mix one part of the second lightest paint color with one part glaze and pour onto a second paper plate. Dip the tip of the spackle knife into the first mixture, and drag the paint randomly across the bricks. *Note: I like to apply more toward the ceiling, floor, and edges.* Repeat this with the second mixture, until desired aged effect is achieved.

*Tip:*

If you would like to deviate from all the bricks being the same size, draw in a few smaller stones as I have. Color them in using a small paintbrush and the technique explained in Step 7.

Step 9

Step 11

Step 12a

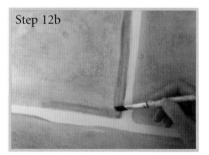

Step 12b

Step 13a

Step 13b

In this example of the Aged Stone Wall, the bricks in the corner are simply painted at a smaller ratio than the ones shown on page 71. The left side of the wall, where the flowerpots hang is real brick—virtually indistinguishable from the faux brick on the right.

# Torn Vellum

Baths and powder rooms provide ideal venues for learning new painting techniques. This finish is light, subtle, and perfect for a small area.

## MATERIALS LIST:

- Latex paint, color of choice
- Paint roller
- Paint tray
- Paintbrush, 1"
- Paper plates
- Sea sponge
- Spackle knife, 6"
- Vellum paper
- Wallpaper paste

*Continued on page 78*

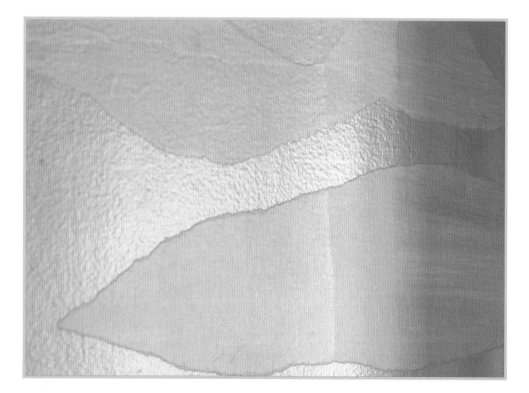

*Continued from page 76*

Step 1.   Using paint roller, paint wall desired color.

Step 2.   Tear vellum paper into uneven strips. Tear any straight edges that will not be adjacent to the ceiling or floor.

Step 3.   Using 1" paintbrush, apply wallpaper paste to one side of the torn velum. Apply vellum to wall, slightly stretching the paper as it is smoothed out. Use the spackle knife to press out all air bubbles from underneath the paper, taking care not to rip the paper. *Note: The vellum will shrink back to its original size as it dries.*

Step 4.   Continue to randomly place paper onto the walls, overlapping two or three pieces together in one area. Repeat until the desired composition is achieved.

Step 5.   Dip dampened sponge into paint, soaking up only a slight amount. Place a light wash over the vellum. Using the clean side of the sponge, soak up any excess paint. Periodically, rinse out the sponge and start over, until a soft and blended look is achieved. Allow to dry. *Note: For a more dramatic look, wash over wall with gold metallic glaze, blending in and feathering to avoid harsh lines.*

Step 6.   Place handwritten words randomly over the collage. Refer to Handwriting Technique on page 16.

Step 2

Step 3

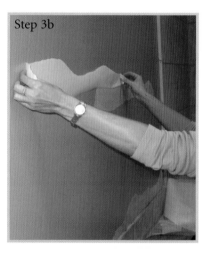
Step 3b

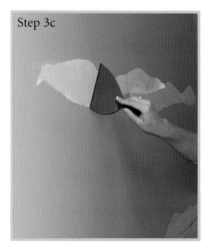
Step 3c

Step 5a

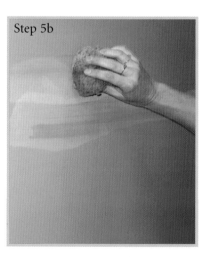
Step 5b

# Watercolor Decoupage

Decoupage was once known as poor man's art, because those who couldn't afford to hire an artist to decorate their furniture could obtain quite elegant effects with cutouts pasted on and covered with multiple coats of varnish or lacquer. This project's finish combines decoupage with watercolor and metallic glazes for an original, inspired wall.

## MATERIALS LIST:

- Acrylic paints, three colors of choice
- Color photocopies: letters, menus, receipts, recipes, wine labels
- Decoupage medium
- Ink pads: gold, pewter
- Metallic glazes: gold, silver

- Paint pens: gold, silver
- Paint trays
- Paintbrushes: 1", 2"–3"
- Rubber stamps
- Sea sponge
- Translucent glaze

*Continued on page 82*

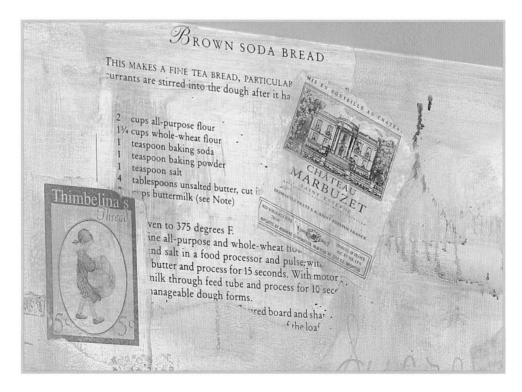

*Continued from page 80*

**Step 1.** Mix one part of first paint color with three parts glaze.

**Step 2.** Using the larger paintbrush, apply mixture to wall. Dip the paintbrush in water, and go over the wet paint, causing runs and drips like watercolor.

**Step 3.** Mix two parts of the second paint color with one part water. Using the 1" brush, flip the paint onto the wall to create splatters. Allow to dry for about one hour.

**Step 4.** Tear around edges of decoupage images. *Note: Don't worry too much about overtearing the images. Slight imperfections will add to your design.*

**Step 5.** Using the 1" brush, coat the back of each image with decoupage medium. Randomly place the images asymmetrically over the wall, wrapping around corners when necessary. *Note: You will also be adding stamps and handwritten words to the wall, so be certain to leave room for these items, as well.* Brush over the tops of all images with a coat of decoupage medium. Allow to dry.

**Step 6.** Mix one part of the last paint color with three parts translucent glaze. Dampen sponge and lightly wash entire decoupaged wall with paint/glaze mixture.

**Step 7.** Dip the very tip of the larger brush into gold metallic glaze, wiping off any excess. Alternating between horizontal and vertical brush strokes, apply to entire wall until the desired look is achieved. Allow to dry.

**Step 8.** Rubber-stamp images into any areas that may need additional color or design, as well as over the decoupaged images.

**Step 9.** Place handwritten words over any areas of the wall that need additional color or design, as well as over the decoupaged images until desired look is achieved. Refer to Handwriting Technique on page 16.

*Tip:*

As all of the paint used in the project has been mixed with water or glaze, it will wash off easily. You can use this to your advantage if you feel too much paint has been applied in any areas. Simply wipe some of the paint off with a wet rag or sponge.

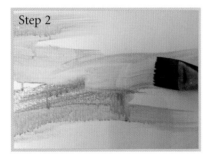
Step 2

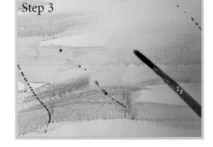
Step 3

Step 6a

Step 6b

Step 7a

Step 7b

# Versatile Textured Wall

This wall finish is the perfect solution for covering slight imperfections or simply adding some fun texture. It can be applied to just about any substrate, requires minimal supplies, and is very easy to do. Various colors can result in a soft, contemporary, elegant, rustic, or whimsical piece.

## MATERIALS LIST:

- Containers, two 2-gallon
- Joint compound, 5 gallons
- Latex paints: three colors of choice
- Paint stirrers
- Satin water-based polyurethane (optional)
- Spoon or sturdy stick
- Trowel, 8"

*Continued on page 86*

*Continued from page 84*

Step 1. Divide the joint compound into three equal parts, placing one-third into each of the two-gallon containers and leaving one-third in the original 5-gallon bucket.

Step 2. Add approximately two cups of the first paint color to one container of joint compound, stirring until completely mixed. *Note: Using a drill mixer to stir the paint into the joint compound will save a great deal of time with the mixing process.* Repeat with the two remaining paint colors and joint compound containers. *Note: If the mixtures are too thin, it will not be able to be applied to the wall.*

Step 3. Using the paint stirrers, place equal amounts of all three paint mixtures onto the trowel.

Step 4. Apply to the wall no more than ⅛" thick in a circular pattern or vertical motion. Work the mixtures together to desired effect. *Note: The more the mixtures are worked together, the cloudier the wall will look.*

Step 5. Allow to dry for 24 hours. *Note: The paint will dry several shades lighter than when wet as a result of mixing with joint compound.*

Optional: Apply one coat of polyurethane to restore the original paint colors, which will also make the wall more durable and washable. Adding additional coats of polyurethane will cause the wall to be much shinier.

Step 1

Step 2

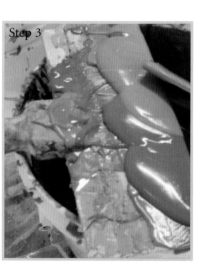
Step 3

Step 4a

Step 4b

Step 4c

This textured wall was created using a mixture of cool greens and neutral beiges, following the technique on pages 84–86; however, no polyurethene was applied. The colors make an excellent backdrop in the photography studio for which the wall was painted.

# Chocolate Countertops

I recently purchased a home that was in need of cosmetic attention. In addition to older cabinets and dated light fixtures, the kitchen had Formica countertops. I wanted to do something unique, that could be hand-painted yet remain durable.

## MATERIALS LIST:

- Acrylic paints: burnt umber, raw sienna
- Assorted alphabet letters: metal, scrabble pieces, scrapbook, stickers
- Butcher paper, enough to cover counter-top one-and-a-half times
- Calking gun and clear silicone
- Countertop trim, countertop thickness plus ¼"
- Decoupage medium
- Metallic papers: copper, gold, silver
- Paintbrushes: #5, ¾"
- Sea sponge
- Superglue
- Surfboard resin/catalyst
- Tape measure

*Continued on page 90*

*Continued from page 88*

After researching and experimenting with various epoxies and resins, I came up with the idea for this basic decoupage covered in surfboard resin. The countertops have proven to be quite resilient, and are oftentimes the topic of conversation in my kitchen. This is one of my favorite projects and a great way to affordably replace out-of-date countertops.

Step 1.   An adequate surface for applying decoupage is necessary for this project. Remove any Formica or tile, or begin with a new plywood or particle board surface.

Step 2.   One quart of surfboard resin will cover 12" x 25" at ¼" thick. Simply measure the length of the countertop to ascertain how many quarts are needed. *Note: I recommend purchasing a few extra quarts in case they are needed.*

Step 3.   Tear the perimeter of all the paper. Tear two-thirds of the paper into large 18"–24" squares and rectangles. *Notes: Tearing the edges makes a more pleasing piece once the paper has been antiqued. The paint adheres to the torn edges, creating a nice effect.*

Step 4.   Apply torn paper over the entire countertop surface, covering any exposed areas. Refer to Decoupage Technique on page 18.

Step 5.   Hand-paint desired wording onto the remaining paper in burnt umber. Refer to Handwriting Technique on page 16. *Note: Following my chosen theme, I painted the word "chocolate" in several different languages, fonts, and sizes.* Allow to dry.

Step 6.   Decoupage hand-painted lettering over the paper-covered surface. Allow to dry for approximately three hours.

Step 7.   Apply raw sienna craft paint in a circular motion, using dampened sea sponge. Make certain to cover all of the paper and wording. If too much paint has been applied, use the other side of the sponge to wipe off any excess. Make certain to not overwork the paint, as it is being washed over a water-soluble decoupage medium that could potentially dissolve with excessive wiping. Allow to dry.

*Continued on page 92*

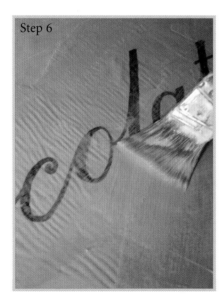

Step 6

Step 7

*Continued from page 90*

Step 8.  Apply various words to the countertop, using the assorted metal, scrabble pieces, scrapbook, and/or sticker letters. *Notes: Those letters that are not self-adhesive can be applied with superglue.*

*I used words such as bittersweet, dark, dessert, cocoa, cake, milk, and fudge to maintain the chocolate theme.*

Step 9.  Cut metallic papers into 1" squares. Apply decoupage medium to the backs of the squares, and adhere in random clusters over the countertop.

Step 10.  Install trim along the front edge of the counter, aligning bottom edges. *Notes: The trim is to prevent the liquid resin from running off the edge of the counter.*

*Self-tapping screws work well for aluminum trim, while construction glue, nails, or wood screws can be used with wooden trim.*

Step 11.  Apply clear silicone along the inside perimeter of the countertop to prevent any resin from seeping into small cracks. Allow to dry for 12–24 hours.

Step 12.  Following package instructions, evenly pour resin across countertop. *Note: The resin will settle evenly on level countertops so make certain to not touch or smooth it, as this will create flaws. Allow approximately 1–2 hours for the resin to set.*

Step 13.  As the resin will shrink away from the walls and trim a slight amount, apply clear silicone to all edges of the countertop to fill in and protect these areas. Allow to dry for 12–24 hours.

*Note: If it is necessary to cut a hole for a sink, simply proceed as with any other kitchen countertop surface. Although the resin creates a durable surface, it can still burn or scratch. It can be scrubbed with nonabrasive cleansers and will hold up well with everyday use.*

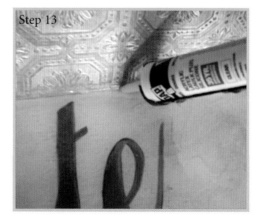

SINFUL

# Damask Table

I found this table at a thrift store, and although it had some stains on the top, it was in fairly good condition. With a little effort, those pieces of furniture that require some fixing up are oftentimes the least expensive, yet most striking. Simply strip off any old paint or varnish, sand, and prime the table's surface.

## MATERIALS LIST:

- Acrylic paint, burnt umber
- Crayon, black, brown, or other dark color
- Metallic paints: gold, silver
- Paint rag
- Paintbrushes: #5, 1½"
- Paper plate
- Patterned fabric
- Satin water-based varnish
- Tissue paper

*Continued on page 96*

*Continued from page 94*

Step 1.  Using the 1½" paintbrush, apply two coats of silver metallic paint to the table. Allow to dry between coats.

Step 2.  Dip the paint rag into the gold metallic paint. Rub over the table in a circular motion, allowing some of the silver to show through. Allow to dry.

Step 3.  Draw the fabric pattern onto a sheet of tissue paper, using the crayon. Refer to Handwriting Technique on page 16. Transfer the image to the table.

Step 4.  Using the #5 paintbrush, paint the artwork gold. *Note: It may take two to three coats to attain the desired effect.* Allow to dry for about one hour.

Step 5.  Mix one part burnt umber craft paint with two parts gold metallic paint. Outline the artwork for added dimension and allow to dry.

Step 6.  Apply 2–3 coats varnish to painted areas of the table. Allow to dry between coats, referring to manufacturer's instructions for specific drying times.

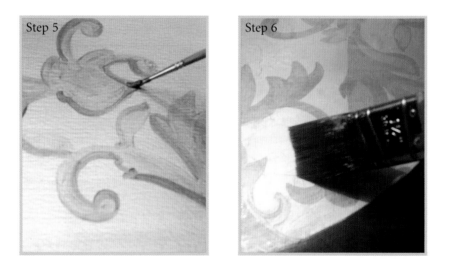

# Rusty Metal Wall

The painting techniques that I find to be the most fun and forgiving are those that represent an aged look. This wall is meant to look like the rusted inside of an old steel ship.

## MATERIALS LIST:

- Acrylic paint, black
- Latex paints, two colors of choice
- Metallic paint, copper
- Paint roller
- Paint tray

- Paintbrush, 2"
- Paper plates
- Sea sponge
- Squeeze bottle
- Styrofoam applicator

Step 1.   Using a roller, paint the walls the desired base color. Allow to dry for at least four hours.

Step 2.   Dip the 2" paintbrush into the black craft paint, wiping off as much excess as possible to allow for a dry-brush effect. Apply paint to the wall in random areas, using both vertical and horizontal brush-strokes. Allow to dry.

Step 3.   Pour metallic copper paint onto a paper plate and pick up a slight amount with the Styrofoam applicator. Beginning at the top of the wall, vertically drag the applicator down. Pick up more paint as necessary, until the entire wall is randomly covered.

Step 4.   Pour equal amounts of both latex paint colors onto a paper plate. Dip a dampened sea sponge into both colors and dab onto the wall. Vertically drag the sea sponge down, streaking the paint. *Note: There should now be alternating black, copper, and chosen base paint color streaks over the entire wall, overlapping in some areas.*

Step 5.   Mix one part of the second paint color with one part water in the squeeze bottle. Beginning at the top of the wall, squeeze the mixture from the bottle, allowing it to run down. Continue along the entire wall. Allow to dry.

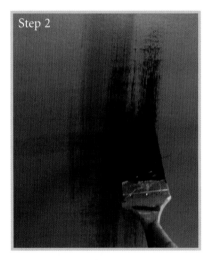

Step 2

Step 3a

Step 3b

Step 4a

Step 4b

Step 5

# Harlequin Floor

This concrete floor was painted for a retail store that sits on a quaint historic street in my hometown. Its eclectic style fits right in with decor and merchandise offered. A creative, inexpensive way to treat an unfinished floor, this technique can be applied to concrete, wood, or even linoleum. The durable and attractive surface is suitable for almost any room.

## MATERIALS LIST:

- Cardboard, sheet large enough to create desired template
- Chalk line or tape measure (optional)
- Concrete paints, three colors of choice
- Light colored pencil
- Masking tape
- Metal ruler
- Metallic paint, gold
- Paint tray

- Paintbrush, 3"
- Paper plates
- Pencil
- Plastic putty knife
- Primer
- Satin water-based varnish
- Sea sponge
- Utility knife

Step 1. Make certain floor is completely clean and free of dust or oil. If the floor has any type of sealer on it, roughly sand or strip it off. *Note: If the floor is not properly prepared, large areas of paint will peel off, especially when removing the tape.*

Step 2. To allow optimal paint adhesion, give the floor a good coat of primer.

Step 3. Pour each color of paint onto a separate paper plate.

Step 4. Dampen the sea sponge, and dip into each of the paint colors so that all three are on the sponge.

*Continued on page 102*

*Continued from page 100*

Step 5. Dab the sponge against the floor, moving and mixing the paint colors only slightly. Make certain to not overwork the area, as the separation of the three colors is desired. Repeat this process until the floor is covered, alternating the amount of paint colors on the sponge each time. *Note: This will prevent the floor from looking uniform, allowing for darker and lighter areas interacting across the floor.*

Step 6. Allow to dry at least overnight; however, it is best to allow the floor to cure for 2–3 days.

Step 7. Enlarge the Diamond Template. *Note: My template measured 18" x 28".* Trace onto the cardboard piece, and cut out using the metal ruler and utility knife.

Step 8. As the pattern is placed randomly over the floor, there is no need to begin in any particular area. *Note: It is recommended that a tape measure or chalk line be used to ensure the template is parallel to the wall to avoid crooked diamonds. Once the first diamond has been correctly placed, the rest will follow suit.*

Step 9. Place the stencil in the desired area and trace around it, using the light colored pencil. Repeat this process until your desired design in complete.

Step 10. Tape off the outside of the diamonds. Run the plastic putty knife along all edges of the tape to secure it to the floor and prevent paint from seeping underneath.

Step 11. Mix one part of the lightest paint color with one part gold metallic paint.

Step 12. Paint one diamond with the metallic paint mixture and allow to dry. Apply a second coat.

Step 13. Remove the tape as quickly as possible, even if the paint is still wet. *Note: The sooner the tape is removed, the easier it will be to pull up.*

Step 14. Repeat Steps 11–12 until all of the diamonds are painted in. *Note: It is not necessary to seal the floor, although it is certainly acceptable if you wish. Simply roll one or two coats of water-based varnish across the floor with a paint roller and extension pole, allowing it to dry according to manufacturer's instructions. The example shown in the photograph, however, has not had any problems with chipping or peeling, despite being inside a retail store.*

*Note: This technique can be applied to nearly any type of floor surface. Instead of concrete paint, I used deck stain to create the same effect and liven up my backyard.*

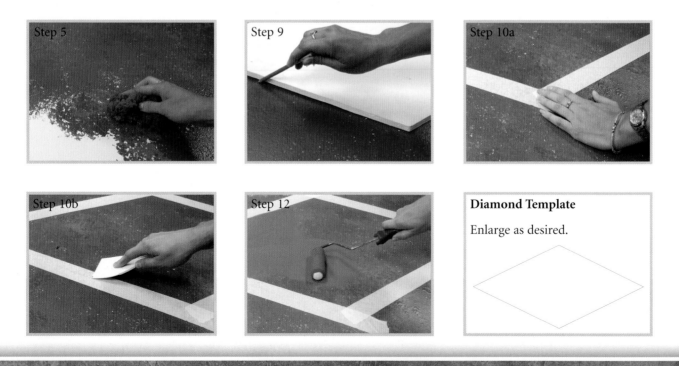

Step 5

Step 9

Step 10a

Step 10b

Step 12

**Diamond Template**

Enlarge as desired.

The Harlequin Floor makes a beautiful statement indoors or out. Instead of using concrete paint, I used deck stain to create the same effect while livening up my backyard. Although subtly painted, the detail is still striking.

# *Faux Leather Travel Room*

I recently planned a trip to New York City and wanted to have something special to always remind me of the great time I had. I designed this guest room around my travels and dedicated one wall to New York. It just seemed appropriate to show the city skyline with an exaggerated Empire State Building. The background for each wall is faux leather, to replicate old suitcases.

## MATERIALS LIST:

- Acrylic paint, burnt umber
- Artist's paintbrushes, assorted sizes including ½"
- Artwork, enlarged to size of wall
- Household cleaner
- Latex paint, color of choice
- Level
- Paint rollers
- Paint trays
- Paintbrushes, 1", 4"
- Paper plates
- Pencil
- Plastic container, quart-size
- Plastic drop cloth, .7mm
- Scissors
- Stippling brush
- Translucent glaze
- Wallpaper paste
- Water-based wood stains, two colors of choice

*Continued on page 106*

*Continued from page 104*

*Note: I had my artwork enlarged and printed at a blueprint store, although any shop that specializes in making large reproductions can help you.*

**Wall**

Step 1.  Cut out printed artwork images, if possible, leaving it in one large piece.

Step 2.  Coat the back side of the image with wallpaper paste and apply to the wall. *Note: Since this is not actually wallpaper, the paper will tear easily once the paste has been applied. Make certain that the image does not have to be repositioned once placed on the wall.*

Step 3.  Using your hands or a large paintbrush, begin in the center of the image and press all of the air bubbles out from beneath the paper. Allow to dry for at least two hours.

Step 4.  Dip a 1" paintbrush into the latex paint and blend the tops of the artwork. Brush unevenly down into the artwork creating an impressionistic feel. Allow to dry.

**Faux leather**

Step 5.  Cut the plastic drop cloth into 3'-square pieces. *Note: Several of these squares will be used, as they should be thrown out once they become too messy to work with.*

*Continued on page 108*

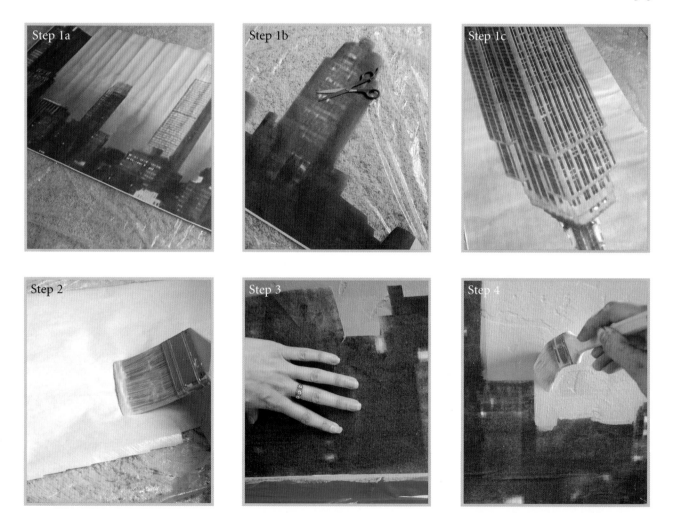

Step 1a

Step 1b

Step 1c

Step 2

Step 3

Step 4

*Continued from page 106*

**Step 6.** Mix one part of the first wood stain with one part translucent glaze. Pour into a paint tray.

**Step 7.** Working in 6'-wide floor-to-ceiling sections, roll the first stain/glaze mixture onto the wall the same as when applying latex paint to a wall. *Notes: Due to the fairly quick drying time, it is imperative that the work be done in sections. The mixture can be rolled over the artwork, as well, creating an aged look that blends nicely with the leather walls.*

**Step 8.** Using the stippling brush to dab at the edges of the stain so that it feathers into the painted area of the wall. *Note: If the edges of the stain and paint are not feathered together, a hard line will appear once you move to the next section of the wall.*

**Step 9.** Repeat Steps 7–8 until entire wall is covered.

**Step 10.** Mix one part of the second wood stain with one part translucent glaze and pour into the plastic container. Using the 4" brush, randomly apply over the rolled stain/glaze mixture.

**Step 11.** Use the stippling brush to blend the two stain mixtures together. *Note: This step is imperative for creating the random light/dark shades in real leather.*

**Step 12.** *Note: Steps 12–13 should not be applied over the artwork, just the background areas of the wall. However, it is not necessary to tape off or cover up the artwork, as it will be fine if some minor overlapping occurs.* Crinkle one piece of plastic and dab against the first stain mixture that was applied to the wall. Rotate the plastic or recrinkle with each dab to prevent a pattern from forming. Continue until the entire wall has been treated.

*Continued on page 110*

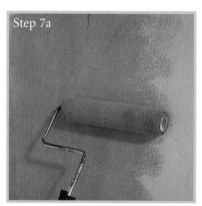

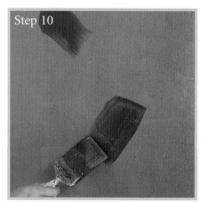

*Continued from page 108*

Step 13. Immediately use the stippling brush to dab against the crinkled areas of the wall. Allow to dry, for approximately two hours.

**Mural**

Step 14. Pour small amounts of latex and burnt umber craft paints onto a paper plate. Using the ½" artist's brush, paint over some of the lighter areas of the image applied to the wall. Using just the burnt umber, paint over some of the darker areas. *Note: By not being too exact, the hand-painted, impressionistic feel is achieved.*

Step 15. Use the level to lightly pencil in random straight lines over the faux-finished leather background.

Step 16. Use an artist's brush and the second wood stain/ glaze mixture to hand-paint in words associated with the theme of the mural. *Note: If freehand painting the words on the wall seems intimidating, print words in desired font. Refer to Handwriting Technique on page 16.* Allow to dry.

Step 17. Using a household cleaner, clean off all of the pencil lines.

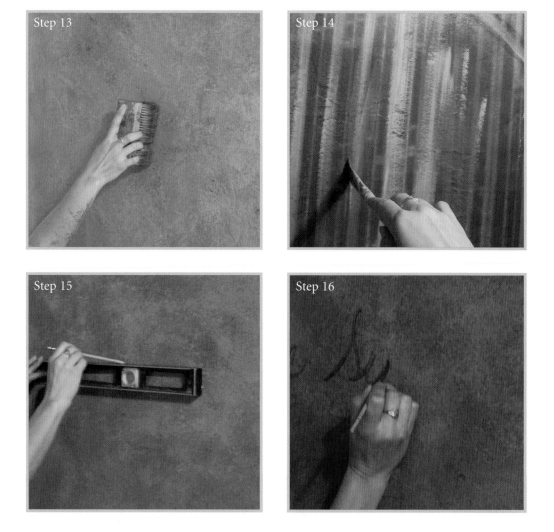

# Confetti Wall

This is a festive wall finish that would work just as well in a children's space as in a den. The intense green colors along with the copper metallic glaze make for a warm, cheerful room.

## MATERIALS LIST:

- Acrylic antiquing glaze
- Antiquing glaze
- Assorted decorative papers
- Decoupage medium
- Latex paints, two colors of choice
- Metallic glaze, copper

- Paint rag
- Paintbrushes: 1", 3"
- Paper plates
- Styrofoam applicator
- Spray paint, black

Step 1. Paint wall desired background color.

Step 2. Pour the second paint color onto a paper plate. Dampen the Styrofoam applicator with water, and pick up a dab of paint. Apply to wall in a wiping motion. Rewet the Styrofoam applicator with water as necessary. *Note: Dampening the applicator will help the paint spread more easily.*

Step 3. Dampen the 3" paintbrush with water, and pick up some of the same paint color used in the previous step. Go back over the wall with paint in a crisscross pattern. Allow to dry for one hour. *Note: Some areas of the wall will be darker and more blended.*

Step 4. Using the same crisscross motion, apply copper metallic glaze in random areas on the wall. Allow to dry.

Step 5. Using a paint rag, wipe antiquing glaze over the entire wall and allow to dry. *Note: The antiquing glaze will deepen the colors and give the wall a richer feel.*

Step 6. Cut the assorted decorative papers into 1"–1½" squares and rectangles.

Step 7. Using the 1" paintbrush, apply decoupage medium to the backs of the cut papers. Apply randomly, in clusters, over entire wall.

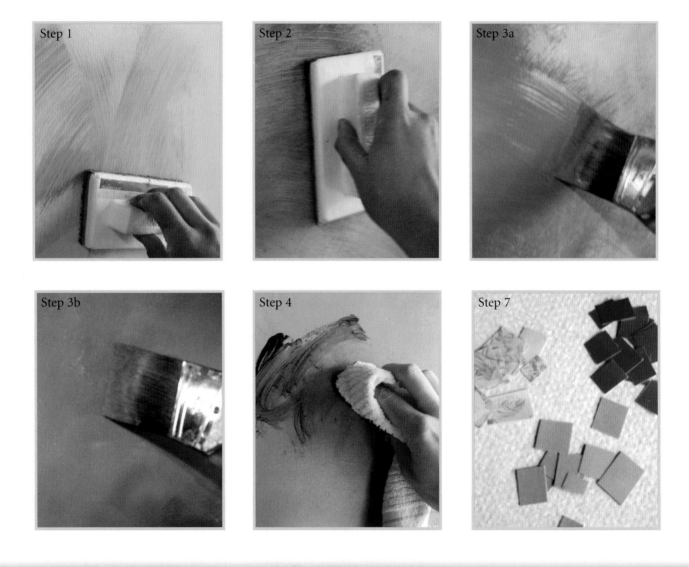

Step 1

Step 2

Step 3a

Step 3b

Step 4

Step 7

# SECTION 2
## *The Gallery*

This faux finish, done in warm tones of yellow and orange, brings a touch of rustic elegance to this dining room. A small amount of a darker shade of paint was put on the edge of a trowel and dragged down along edges, corners, and where the wall meets floor to yield an aged look.

The white-washed brick faux finish on this hanging panel adds to the charm of this topiary-themed sitting area. It was applied using a variation on the technique for the Aged Stone Wall on pages 70–75.

The wall above this romantic bedroom fireplace was antiqued with two shades of antiquing glaze, creating a frame around the outside with the darker shade. A hand-painted jewelry box was the inspiration for the subtle leaf design painted along the inside edge of the frame.

The wet bar in this home needed some detail to spice up the room.
The hand-painted squares emulate the the look of the brick path
featured in the painting, creating the feeling of Italian tile.

These used to be ordinary, white flat-panel doors. To give them depth and warmth, I added a few picture frames and applied an oak faux wood finish on the doors with a burl finish within the frames.

jutsu _Japanese_

KONST _Swedish_

じゆつ _Japanese Characters_

ARTE _Spanish_

A
R
T

This wall was created for an office, displaying the word "Art" in several languages. Quite simple to create, it involves simple painting and applying the Handwriting Technique on page 16.

# Author's Recommendations

Many people like to choose the colors or brands for their projects based on personal preference and availability. However, for those wishing to duplicate my projects, here is a list of some of the products that were used throughout this book.

**Aged Stone Wall on pages 70–75**

Lowe's American Tradition Signature Colors in Basalt, Bison Brown, Canvas, Cocoa Rose, Khaki, Soft Brick, and Truffle

**Ancestral Armoire on pages 47–49**

Behr latex paint in Off-white

Behr Premium Plus with Style metallic glaze in Gold

**Artichoke Headboard on pages 43–46**

Apple Barrel acrylic paints in Antique White, Black, Burnt Umber, Leaf Green, Lime Yellow, Olive Green, and Terra Cotta

Ambassador latex paint in Calico Doublec

Minwax water-based stains in Bombay Mahogany, Colonial Pine, and Early American

Shurline Styrofoam applicator

**Artist's Textured Wall on pages 26–29**

Behr latex paint in New Brick

Goop industrial-strength adhesive

Flexall patching plaster

**Asian Linen on pages 52–54**

Apple Barrel acrylic paints in Black and Burnt Umber

Behr latex paints in Bavarian Cream, Chianti, and New Brick

Behr Premium Plus with Style metallic paint in Gold

Shurline Styrofoam applicator

**Canvas Mural on pages 34–35**

Liquid Nails construction glue

**Chocolate Countertops on pages 88–93**

Apple Barrel acrylic paint in Burnt Umber

Waterclear surfboard resin and catalyst: http://www.tapplastics.com

**Confetti Wall on pages 111–113**

Behr latex paints in Celery Sprig and Moss Landing

Behr Premium Plus metallic glaze in Copper

**Damask Table on pages 94–96**

Apple Barrel acrylic paint in Burnt Umber

Behr Premium Plus with Style metallic paints in Gold and Silver

**Faux Leather Travel Room on pages 104–110**

Apple Barrel acrylic paint in Burnt Umber

Behr latex paint in Wilmington Tan

Minwax water-based stains in American Walnut and Colonial Pine

**Greek Architecture on pages 60–63**

Behr latex paints in Antique White, Ashwood, and Bavarian Cream

**Harlequin Floor on pages 100–103**

Behr concrete paints in Suede Chaps, Copper Top, and Cold Lager

Behr Premium Plus metallic paint in Gold

**Metallic Harlequin Wall on pages 64–69**

American Tradition latex paint in Twilight Mist

Behr latex paints in Pixie Violet, Ruffled Iris, and Silver

Liquitex interference paint in Violet

Behr Premium Plus metallic glaze in Silver

Goop industrial-strength adhesive

**Metallic Tissue Paper Wall on pages 22–25**

Behr latex paints in Gray Morning and Toffee Crunch

Behr Premium Plus with Style metallic paint in Gold

Shurline Styrofoam applicator

**Music Room on pages 50–51**

Behr latex paints in Bavarian Cream and Brown Teepee

**Oriental Sheer on pages 40–42**

Lowe's American Tradition Signature Colors in Midnight Green

**Renaissance Antiqued Mirror on pages 36–39**

Mod Podge decoupage medium

**Rusty Metal Wall on pages 97–99**

Apple Barrel acrylic paint in Black

Behr latex paints in Brick and Mountain Ridge

Behr Premium Plus with Style metallic paint in Copper

Shurline Styrofoam applicator

**Texture Magic Mantel on pages 30–33**

Delta Texture Magic dimensional paint in Almond

**Unfinished Mural on pages 55–59**

Apple Barrel acrylic paints in Burnt Sienna, Cinnamon Apple, Country Tan, Golden Brown, Light Leaf Green, Nutmeg, Olive Green, White, and Wild Berry

Behr latex paints in Marina Isle and Wickerware

Shurline Styrofoam applicator

**Versatile Textured Wall on pages 84–87**

Behr latex paints in Campground, Dark As Night, and Melted Chocolate

**Watercolor Decoupage on pages 80–83**

Apple Barrel acrylic paints in English Ivy, Lavender, and Nutmeg Brown

Behr Premium Plus metallic glazes in Gold and Silver

# About the Author

Suzy Eaton realized her artistic abilities as a small child and has been mastering her technique ever since. She studied art at the University of Utah in Salt Lake City and at Weber State University in Ogden, Utah. She has always worked in the field of art as a graphic designer, a photo stylist, and an artist. She has been applying and instructing the art of faux finishing, murals, and decorative painting for over sixteen years. Although she finds these techniques rewarding, her favorite medium is watercolor. She also enjoys furniture refinishing, remodeling, decorating, and mosaic work. More of her work can be seen at www.suzyeaton.com.

# Acknowledgments

To my dear friend Kelly. Without her unconditional love and support in all aspects of my chaotic life, this book would not be possible.

A special thank-you to my children, Jordan, Danni, and Connor, for their relentless patience with my never-ending "projects" and for allowing me to pursue my dreams.

To my editor Ana Maria Ventura for pulling it all together and producing something wonderful. Thank-you to my photographer and friend Zachary Williams for his keen eye and always-positive attitude.

# Credits

Book Editor: Ana Maria Ventura

Copy Editor: Marilyn Goff

Book Designer: Tony Olsen

Photographer: Zac Williams for Chapelle Ltd.

Photo Stylist: Suzy Eaton

Graphic Designer: Tony Olsen

# Metric Equivalency Charts

## MM-MILLIMETERS CM-CENTIMETERS
## INCHES TO MILLIMETERS AND CENTIMETERS

| INCHES | MM | CM | INCHES | CM | INCHES | CM |
|---|---|---|---|---|---|---|
| ⅛ | 3 | 0.3 | 9 | 22.9 | 30 | 76.2 |
| ¼ | 6 | 0.6 | 10 | 25.4 | 31 | 78.7 |
| ½ | 13 | 1.3 | 12 | 30.5 | 33 | 83.8 |
| ⅝ | 16 | 1.6 | 13 | 33.0 | 34 | 86.4 |
| ¾ | 19 | 1.9 | 14 | 35.6 | 35 | 88.9 |
| ⅞ | 22 | 2.2 | 15 | 38.1 | 36 | 91.4 |
| 1 | 25 | 2.5 | 16 | 40.6 | 37 | 94.0 |
| 1¼ | 32 | 3.2 | 17 | 43.2 | 38 | 96.5 |
| 1½ | 38 | 3.8 | 18 | 45.7 | 39 | 99.1 |
| 1¾ | 44 | 4.4 | 19 | 48.3 | 40 | 101.6 |
| 2 | 51 | 5.1 | 20 | 50.8 | 41 | 104.1 |
| 2½ | 64 | 6.4 | 21 | 53.3 | 42 | 106.7 |
| 3 | 76 | 7.6 | 22 | 55.9 | 43 | 109.2 |
| 3½ | 89 | 8.9 | 23 | 58.4 | 44 | 111.8 |
| 4 | 102 | 10.2 | 24 | 61.0 | 45 | 114.3 |
| 4½ | 114 | 11.4 | 25 | 63.5 | 46 | 116.8 |
| 5 | 127 | 12.7 | 26 | 66.0 | 47 | 119.4 |
| 6 | 152 | 15.2 | 27 | 68.6 | 48 | 121.9 |
| 7 | 178 | 17.8 | 28 | 71.1 | 49 | 124.5 |
| 8 | 203 | 20.3 | 29 | 73.7 | 50 | 127.0 |

## YARDS TO METERS

| YARDS | METERS | YARDS | METERS | YARDS | METERS | YARDS | METERS | YARDS | METERS |
|---|---|---|---|---|---|---|---|---|---|
| ⅛ | 0.11 | 2⅛ | 1.94 | 4⅛ | 3.77 | 6⅛ | 5.60 | 8⅛ | 7.43 |
| ¼ | 0.23 | 2¼ | 2.06 | 4¼ | 3.89 | 6¼ | 5.72 | 8¼ | 7.54 |
| ⅜ | 0.34 | 2⅜ | 2.17 | 4⅜ | 4.00 | 6⅜ | 5.83 | 8⅜ | 7.66 |
| ½ | 0.46 | 2½ | 2.29 | 4½ | 4.11 | 6½ | 5.94 | 8½ | 7.77 |
| ⅝ | 0.57 | 2⅝ | 2.40 | 4⅝ | 4.23 | 6⅝ | 6.06 | 8⅝ | 7.89 |
| ¾ | 0.69 | 2¾ | 2.51 | 4¾ | 4.34 | 6¾ | 6.17 | 8¾ | 8.00 |
| ⅞ | 0.80 | 2⅞ | 2.63 | 4⅞ | 4.46 | 6⅞ | 6.29 | 8⅞ | 8.12 |
| 1 | 0.91 | 3 | 2.74 | 5 | 4.57 | 7 | 6.40 | 9 | 8.23 |
| 1⅛ | 1.03 | 3⅛ | 2.86 | 5⅛ | 4.69 | 7⅛ | 6.52 | 9⅛ | 8.34 |
| 1¼ | 1.14 | 3¼ | 2.97 | 5¼ | 4.80 | 7¼ | 6.63 | 9¼ | 8.46 |
| 1⅜ | 1.26 | 3⅜ | 3.09 | 5⅜ | 4.91 | 7⅜ | 6.74 | 9⅜ | 8.57 |
| 1½ | 1.37 | 3½ | 3.20 | 5½ | 5.03 | 7½ | 6.86 | 9½ | 8.69 |
| 1⅝ | 1.49 | 3⅝ | 3.31 | 5⅝ | 5.14 | 7⅝ | 6.97 | 9⅝ | 8.80 |
| 1¾ | 1.60 | 3¾ | 3.43 | 5¾ | 5.26 | 7¾ | 7.09 | 9¾ | 8.92 |
| 1⅞ | 1.71 | 3⅞ | 3.54 | 5⅞ | 5.37 | 7⅞ | 7.20 | 9⅞ | 9.03 |
| 2 | 1.83 | 4 | 3.66 | 6 | 5.49 | 8 | 7.32 | 10 | 9.14 |

# Index

THE

CHOCOLATE

BIBLE

The Definitive Sourcebook,
with over 600
Illustrations

Christian Teubner

dessert

DARK

Choco